The Pomegranate Grower's Handbook

The Ultimate Guide to Growing and Caring For Delicious

Pomegranates Like a Pro!!

DID YOU KNOW

"

Pomegranates thrive in warm climates with hot summers and mild winters. They are drought-tolerant and can grow in regions with minimal water resources.

"

Table of Contents

Chapter 19: Pomegranate Recipes for Every Occasion

Chapter 20: Additional Resources

How to Grow and Care For
Pomegranate

Chapter 1

Introduction to Pomegranates

Pomegranates have a long and rich history that spans continents and centuries. Known for their jewel-like seeds and vibrant flavor, pomegranates have captured the attention of cultures around the world. This fruit is not only celebrated for its delicious taste but also revered for its numerous health benefits and symbolic significance. As gardeners and food enthusiasts continue to explore the world of pomegranates, understanding their background and importance is essential.

History and Origins of Pomegranates

Pomegranates have a storied past that dates back thousands of years, making them one of the oldest known fruits cultivated by humankind. The origins of the pomegranate are believed to trace back to the region encompassing modern-day Iran and Northern India. Archaeological evidence suggests that the fruit was cultivated as early as 3000 BCE, with its popularity spreading to neighboring regions through trade routes. Pomegranates were quickly embraced by ancient civilizations, including the Egyptians, Greeks, and Romans, who considered them a symbol of prosperity and abundance.

In ancient Egypt, pomegranates were so highly prized that they were buried with the dead as offerings for the afterlife. Egyptian art and artifacts often depict the fruit, highlighting its revered status. Similarly, in Greek mythology, pomegranates played a crucial role in the tale of Persephone and Hades. The fruit's seeds were said to have bound Persephone to the underworld, symbolizing the cyclical nature of life and death. The Greeks associated pomegranates with fertility, and they became an essential part of rituals and ceremonies.

As pomegranates continued to spread across the Mediterranean and into Europe, their influence expanded. Roman culture adopted the fruit as a symbol of power and wealth, and it was frequently depicted in art and architecture. The Romans introduced pomegranates to the Iberian Peninsula, where the fruit became integral to Spanish culture. The city of Granada, named after the pomegranate, became a hub for pomegranate cultivation in the region.

The Silk Road trade route played a significant role in spreading pomegranates to the Far East, where the fruit became a cherished commodity. In China, pomegranates were associated with longevity and prosperity, and they were often featured in wedding ceremonies to symbolize a fruitful union. Similarly, in India, the fruit was linked to health and vitality, often used in traditional medicine and Ayurvedic practices.

Throughout history, pomegranates have remained a symbol of abundance, fertility, and prosperity. Their global reach and cultural significance have solidified their place in the history of agriculture and human civilization. From the ancient tombs of Egypt to the bustling markets of Persia, pomegranates have continued to captivate people across the world.

Varieties and Cultivars: Choosing the Right Pomegranate

With over 500 known varieties, pomegranates offer a wide range of flavors, colors, and growth characteristics. These varieties are cultivated in regions with diverse climates, allowing gardeners to select the pomegranate that best suits their environment and taste preferences. While pomegranates are known for their deep red seeds, varieties can range in color from light pink to deep purple, and their flavor profiles can vary from sweet to tangy.

One of the most popular and widely grown pomegranate varieties is the 'Wonderful' cultivar, known for its large, ruby-red arils (seeds) and sweet-tart flavor. This variety thrives in Mediterranean climates, making it a top choice for commercial growers in California, Spain, and Israel. The 'Wonderful' pomegranate is also favored for its high juice content, making it ideal for producing pomegranate juice and other processed products.

For those looking for a sweeter option, the 'Angel Red' variety offers a milder, less tart flavor. The seeds of 'Angel Red' are smaller and softer, making them more enjoyable to eat fresh. This variety is also an excellent choice for those in cooler climates, as it is more cold-tolerant than some other cultivars. Additionally, 'Angel Red' produces fruit earlier in the season, providing an extended harvest window.

The 'Parfianka' variety is prized for its exceptional flavor and versatility. Known for its balance of sweetness and acidity, 'Parfianka' is often regarded as one of the best-tasting pomegranates. Its medium-sized seeds are surrounded by soft arils, making it an excellent choice for fresh consumption. 'Parfianka' is also a reliable producer in a variety of climates, making it a favorite among home gardeners and orchardists.

For those interested in ornamental varieties, the 'Nana' dwarf pomegranate is a popular choice. While the fruit of the 'Nana' is smaller and less flavorful than other varieties, the plant's compact size and attractive flowers make it a favorite for container gardening and landscape design. The 'Nana' pomegranate can be grown indoors or outdoors, offering flexibility for gardeners with limited space.

When selecting a pomegranate variety, it is essential to consider factors such as climate, soil conditions, and intended use. Some varieties are better suited for juice production, while others excel as fresh-eating fruits. By choosing the right variety, gardeners can ensure a successful and rewarding pomegranate-growing experience.

Nutritional Profile and Health Benefits

Pomegranates are not only delicious but also packed with essential nutrients and antioxidants that contribute to overall health. Rich in vitamins, minerals, and plant compounds, pomegranates have been hailed as a superfood with a wide range of health benefits. From boosting heart health to supporting immune function, the nutritional profile of pomegranates makes them a valuable addition to a balanced diet.

One of the standout features of pomegranates is their high concentration of antioxidants, particularly polyphenols such as punicalagins and anthocyanins. These powerful antioxidants help combat oxidative stress in the body, reducing the risk of chronic diseases such as heart disease, cancer, and diabetes. Studies have shown that the antioxidant activity in pomegranate juice is higher than that of red wine or green tea, making it an excellent choice for those looking to increase their intake of protective plant compounds.

Nutritional Profile and Health Benefits of Pomegranate

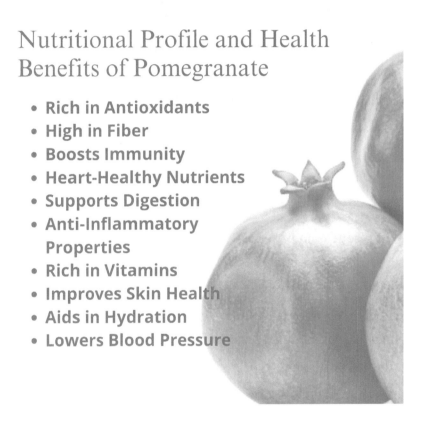

- **Rich in Antioxidants**
- **High in Fiber**
- **Boosts Immunity**
- **Heart-Healthy Nutrients**
- **Supports Digestion**
- **Anti-Inflammatory Properties**
- **Rich in Vitamins**
- **Improves Skin Health**
- **Aids in Hydration**
- **Lowers Blood Pressure**

In addition to antioxidants, pomegranates are a rich source of vitamin C, providing more than 30% of the recommended daily intake in just one serving. Vitamin C is crucial for immune function, skin health, and collagen production. Regular consumption of pomegranates can help support the body's natural defense mechanisms, especially during cold and flu season.

Pomegranates also contain significant amounts of dietary fiber, which is essential for digestive health. The seeds, or arils, provide both soluble and insoluble fiber, aiding in digestion and promoting healthy bowel movements. Fiber is also known to help regulate blood sugar levels and reduce the risk of developing type 2 diabetes, making pomegranates a valuable fruit for maintaining metabolic health.

Pomegranates have been linked to heart health, with studies showing that regular consumption can lower blood pressure, reduce cholesterol levels, and improve overall cardiovascular function. The combination of antioxidants, fiber, and potassium in pomegranates helps protect the heart by reducing inflammation, improving blood flow, and preventing the buildup of plaque in the arteries.

Furthermore, pomegranates have been studied for their potential anti-cancer properties. Research suggests that the antioxidants and bioactive compounds in pomegranates can inhibit the growth of cancer cells and reduce the risk of certain types of cancer, including breast, prostate, and colon cancer. While more research is needed to fully understand the extent of these benefits, pomegranates are widely recognized as a protective food that can support overall health and well-being.

The Pomegranate's Role in Culture and Mythology

Throughout history, pomegranates have been revered not only for their nutritional value but also for their symbolic significance in various cultures and mythologies. From ancient Egypt to modern-day Iran, pomegranates have represented fertility, abundance, and the cycle of life. The fruit's rich symbolism has made it a prominent figure in art, religion, and literature, transcending geographical and cultural boundaries.

In ancient Egypt, pomegranates were considered a symbol of life and death, often placed in tombs as offerings for the deceased. The fruit's many seeds were thought to represent fertility and rebirth, making it a fitting gift for those embarking on their journey to the afterlife. Egyptian art frequently depicted pomegranates in elaborate tomb paintings, highlighting their importance in religious and spiritual practices.

Greek mythology also features the pomegranate prominently, particularly in the story of Persephone and Hades. According to the myth, Persephone, the daughter of Demeter, was kidnapped by Hades and taken to the underworld. While there, she ate a few seeds from a pomegranate, which bound her to the underworld for part of the year. This myth explains the changing seasons, as Demeter, the goddess of agriculture, mourns Persephone's absence during the winter months and rejoices at her return in the spring. The pomegranate, in this context, symbolizes the duality of life and death, as well as the cyclical nature of the seasons.

In Persian culture, the pomegranate is a symbol of love, fertility, and abundance. The fruit is often associated with the goddess Anahita, who is revered as the protector of water, fertility, and women. Pomegranates are also featured in Persian poetry and literature, where they represent beauty, passion, and the richness of life. During Yalda Night, an ancient Persian festival that celebrates the winter solstice, pomegranates are traditionally eaten to symbolize the triumph of light over darkness and the promise of rebirth.

In Jewish tradition, the pomegranate is a symbol of righteousness and knowledge. The fruit is often associated with the Torah, as it is said to contain 613 seeds, representing the 613 commandments of Jewish law. Pomegranates are also used in religious ceremonies and rituals, particularly during the Jewish New Year (Rosh Hashanah), when they are eaten to symbolize the hope for a fruitful and prosperous year ahead.

The pomegranate's influence extends to Christian symbolism as well, where it represents resurrection and eternal life. In Christian art, the fruit is often depicted in the hands of the Virgin Mary or Jesus, symbolizing the promise of eternal salvation. The many seeds of the pomegranate are also seen as a representation of the Church, with its numerous followers united in faith.

Across different cultures and religions, the pomegranate continues to be a powerful symbol of life, fertility, and abundance. Its deep-rooted presence in mythology and culture underscores the fruit's enduring significance throughout human history.

Chapter 2

Selecting the Perfect Site for Your Pomegranate Tree

Pomegranates are resilient plants, but their success hinges on choosing the right location for planting. The environment you create for your tree determines its overall health, growth, and productivity. Whether you're in a warm Mediterranean-like climate or a more temperate region, the key lies in understanding your site's specific needs and potential pitfalls.

Climate Considerations: Understanding Your Growing Zone

Pomegranates thrive in areas with hot, dry summers and cool winters, making them ideally suited to Mediterranean climates. They flourish in USDA hardiness zones 7 through 12, where temperatures typically remain above 10°F (-12°C) during winter. Knowing your specific growing zone is essential for ensuring your pomegranate tree has the right conditions to grow strong and healthy. In colder zones, protective measures, such as using frost cloths or planting against a south-facing wall, can help pomegranates survive.

Regions with long, hot summers and minimal humidity provide the best conditions for pomegranate development. The heat promotes the formation of the sweet, juicy arils that are characteristic of this fruit. However, too much humidity can lead to fungal issues, which may impede growth and fruiting. If you live in a humid area, ensuring proper air circulation around your trees can help mitigate these problems.

Microclimates within your property may also influence your pomegranate's success. For example, areas that receive more sunlight or are shielded from wind may offer more favorable conditions than others. Planting near a heat-retaining structure, such as a brick wall, can create a warmer microclimate that promotes better growth, especially in regions where temperatures dip during winter months.

Temperature fluctuations are another factor to consider. While pomegranates can handle some degree of cold, prolonged exposure to frost can damage the tree's buds and branches. In areas prone to sudden cold snaps, selecting a site that offers some protection from harsh winds and frost pockets can be beneficial. Additionally, elevated areas are less susceptible to frost accumulation, making them suitable for pomegranate planting.

When choosing a site, think about the long-term climate trends in your area. With the increasing unpredictability of weather patterns, ensuring that your chosen location can accommodate changes in temperature and precipitation is wise. Preparing for potential droughts or heavy rains will safeguard your investment and promote your tree's longevity.

Matching the climate conditions of your site with the needs of your pomegranate tree is essential for creating an environment where the plant can flourish. By carefully analyzing your growing zone and microclimate, you can select a site that supports healthy growth and abundant fruit production.

Soil Requirements: Testing and Preparing Your Soil

The soil is the foundation of your pomegranate tree's health, and providing the right conditions for root growth is critical. Pomegranates prefer well-drained soil with a loamy texture, rich in organic matter. While they can tolerate a range of soil types, from sandy to clayey, ensuring that the soil drains well is paramount to preventing root rot and other water-related issues.

Conducting a soil test before planting is highly recommended. Testing provides valuable information about your soil's pH, nutrient levels, and composition, allowing you to amend it as needed. Pomegranates prefer slightly acidic to neutral soils, with a pH range of 5.5 to 7.0. If your soil is too acidic, applying lime can help raise the pH, while sulfur can lower the pH if it is too alkaline.

Adding organic matter, such as compost or well-rotted manure, can significantly improve the soil's fertility and structure. Organic matter enhances soil drainage, increases water retention, and supplies essential nutrients that promote root development. Incorporating a thick layer of compost into the planting area ensures that your pomegranate tree has access to the nutrients it needs during its critical early growth stages.

In areas with heavy clay soil, improving drainage is a priority. Mixing in sand or perlite can help break up dense soil, allowing for better water movement and root penetration. Creating raised beds or mounds can also improve drainage, particularly in regions prone to waterlogging.

Pomegranates arc relatively drought-tolerant once established, but well-drained soil is crucial for young trees as they develop their root systems.

If your soil is excessively sandy, incorporating organic matter will help retain moisture and provide a steady supply of nutrients. Sandy soils can dry out quickly, leading to water stress in pomegranate trees, particularly during hot summer months. Applying mulch around the base of the tree can help conserve moisture and regulate soil temperature.

Soil preparation should begin well before planting to ensure that your site is ready to support healthy growth. Amending the soil with the right materials and ensuring proper drainage will set the stage for a thriving pomegranate tree that can withstand varying weather conditions and nutrient demands.

Sunlight and Watering Needs

Pomegranates are sun-loving plants that require full sunlight to produce abundant, high-quality fruit. Ideally, pomegranate trees should receive at least six to eight hours of direct sunlight per day. Adequate sunlight promotes photosynthesis, leading to vigorous growth and the development of sweet, flavorful arils. When selecting a planting site, prioritize locations that receive uninterrupted sunlight throughout the day, as shaded areas may result in fewer fruits and weaker growth.

Sunlight exposure not only influences the tree's growth but also impacts its resistance to diseases and pests. Plants that receive insufficient sunlight are more susceptible to fungal infections, particularly in humid climates. Full sunlight helps to dry out excess moisture on leaves and branches, reducing the likelihood of fungal growth. In cooler regions, sunlight also plays a vital role in preventing frost damage by warming the tree during the day.

Pomegranates thrive in full sun for abundant, high-quality fruit.

Watering is another critical aspect of pomegranate care, especially during the tree's establishment phase. While pomegranates are drought-tolerant once mature, young trees require regular watering to develop strong root systems. Deep, infrequent watering encourages roots to grow deeper into the soil, enhancing the tree's drought resilience. When watering, ensure that the soil is thoroughly moistened but not waterlogged, as excess moisture can lead to root rot.

Drip irrigation systems are particularly effective for pomegranate trees, as they deliver water directly to the root zone while minimizing evaporation.

This method also helps prevent water from sitting on the foliage, reducing the risk of fungal diseases. If using overhead sprinklers, water early in the day to allow the foliage to dry before nightfall.

As the tree matures, its water needs will decrease, but regular watering during the growing season remains essential for fruit development. Pomegranates produce their best fruit when they receive consistent moisture during the flowering and fruiting periods. However, be cautious not to overwater, as this can cause the fruit to split or lead to root-related issues.

Striking the right balance between sunlight and water is key to ensuring that your pomegranate tree thrives. With adequate light and carefully managed watering practices, your tree will be well-positioned to produce healthy, delicious fruit year after year.

Common Mistakes in Site Selection

Selecting the wrong site for your pomegranate tree can lead to various challenges that affect its growth and productivity. One common mistake is choosing a location with poor drainage. Pomegranates do not tolerate standing water, and planting in a low-lying area or near a waterlogged spot can quickly lead to root rot. Always assess the drainage capabilities of your chosen site and make amendments or adjustments if necessary.

Another mistake is underestimating the importance of sunlight. While pomegranates are adaptable, they will not thrive in shaded or partially shaded areas. Insufficient sunlight can stunt growth, reduce fruit production, and make the tree more vulnerable to pests and diseases. Avoid planting near tall structures or trees that may cast shadows over your pomegranate tree during peak sunlight hours.

Ignoring the microclimate of your property can also lead to suboptimal site selection. Factors such as wind exposure, frost pockets, and temperature fluctuations can have a significant impact on your tree's health. For example, planting in a wind-prone area can lead to broken branches or damaged fruit. Identifying sheltered spots, such as near a fence or wall, can provide some protection from harsh winds.

Spacing is another critical consideration that is often overlooked. Crowding your pomegranate tree too close to other plants or structures can limit its access to sunlight, water, and nutrients. Proper spacing allows for adequate air circulation, which is essential for preventing fungal diseases. Make sure to leave enough room for your tree to grow to its full mature size without interference from neighboring plants or buildings.

Some gardeners also fail to consider the long-term implications of their site's soil quality. Poor soil that has not been properly amended can lead to nutrient deficiencies and slow growth. Taking the time to improve the soil before planting can prevent future problems and ensure that your tree has access to the nutrients it needs to thrive.

Chapter 3

Planting Your Pomegranate Tree

Proper planting is the first step toward a thriving pomegranate tree. A well-planted tree will establish itself more quickly, grow stronger, and produce fruit more reliably. Each stage of the planting process, from timing to spacing, requires careful attention to detail to ensure the best possible outcome for your tree.

Choosing the Right Time to Plant

Timing is crucial when it comes to planting pomegranates. In most climates, the best time to plant a pomegranate tree is during the dormant season, typically in late winter or early spring. This allows the tree to establish its root system before the onset of hot summer weather. In areas with mild winters, pomegranates can also be planted in the fall, giving the tree several months to root before the growing season begins.

Planting during the dormant season minimizes transplant shock and reduces the risk of heat stress. When temperatures are cooler, the tree can focus its energy on root development rather than trying to support new leaf and fruit growth. Avoid planting during the peak of summer, as the intense heat can make it difficult for the tree to establish itself and may lead to dehydration and sunburn.

Consider the specific conditions of your region when determining the best planting time. In frost-prone areas, wait until the danger of frost has passed before planting. Planting too early in the season can expose the tree to cold temperatures that may damage its buds and roots. On the other hand, in regions with hot, dry summers, planting in early spring ensures that the tree has time to establish before the heat sets in.

Container-grown pomegranate trees offer more flexibility in planting time compared to bare-root trees. If you're planting a tree that has been grown in a container, it can be transplanted at almost any time of the year, provided that the soil conditions are favorable and the tree receives adequate water. However, the dormant season is still the preferred time to plant, as it gives the tree the best chance of thriving.

When selecting the right planting time, also consider the availability of water. Newly planted pomegranate trees require consistent moisture to establish their roots. Planting during a season when water is readily available, either through natural rainfall or irrigation, will help support healthy growth.

Choosing the optimal planting time ensures that your pomegranate tree gets off to a strong start. By paying attention to your region's climate and the tree's specific needs, you can create the conditions necessary for successful establishment and long-term growth.

Step-by-Step Planting Guide

The planting process begins with site preparation. Start by digging a hole that is twice as wide and as deep as the root ball of your pomegranate tree. This allows the roots to spread out and establish themselves more easily in the surrounding soil. If you're planting multiple trees, make sure to space the holes far enough apart to accommodate their mature size.

Planting Pomegranate Tree

Once the hole is prepared, carefully remove the tree from its container, taking care not to damage the roots. If the roots are tightly bound or circling the root ball, gently loosen them with your fingers to encourage outward growth. Place the tree in the hole so that the top of the root ball is level with the surrounding soil. Avoid planting too deeply, as this can lead to root rot and other issues.

Backfill the hole with the soil you removed, mixing in organic matter such as compost to improve soil fertility and structure. As you fill in the hole, gently tamp down the soil to eliminate air pockets that could dry out the roots. Water the tree thoroughly after planting to help settle the soil and ensure that the roots make good contact with the surrounding soil.

Mulching around the base of the tree is highly recommended. A 2- to 3-inch layer of mulch helps retain moisture, suppress weeds, and regulate soil temperature. Keep the mulch a few inches away from the trunk to prevent moisture buildup and rot. Organic mulches, such as wood chips or straw, gradually break down and improve soil fertility over time.

Watering is critical during the first few weeks after planting. Deep watering helps the roots establish themselves and encourages deep root growth. Depending on your climate, you may need to water your newly planted tree every few days to ensure it doesn't dry out. Monitoring soil moisture levels will help you adjust your watering schedule as needed.

Staking your tree may be necessary if it is planted in a windy location or if the trunk is weak. Use soft ties to secure the tree to a sturdy stake, ensuring that the tree has enough flexibility to move slightly in the wind. This movement encourages the tree to develop a strong trunk, reducing the need for long-term staking.

By following these detailed steps, you can ensure that your pomegranate tree is planted correctly and has the best chance of thriving. Taking the time to prepare the site and provide proper care during the early stages of growth will set your tree up for long-term success.

Spacing and Layout for Optimal Growth

Proper spacing is essential for the healthy development of your pomegranate tree. Pomegranates require enough room to spread their branches and roots without competing with nearby plants for sunlight, water, and nutrients. The spacing you choose will also influence air circulation around the tree, which is critical for preventing diseases and ensuring robust fruit production.

For single pomegranate trees, a minimum spacing of 12 to 15 feet is recommended. This allows the tree to reach its full size without interference from neighboring trees or structures. In a home garden, this spacing also provides enough room for you to access the tree for pruning, harvesting, and maintenance. In smaller spaces, pomegranate trees can be pruned to maintain a more compact shape, but they will still need sufficient room for sunlight and air circulation.

When planting multiple trees, consider the overall layout of your orchard or garden. Rows of pomegranate trees should be spaced at least 15 feet apart to allow for easy movement between the trees and to provide each tree with adequate sunlight. This layout also helps facilitate airflow, reducing the risk of fungal diseases that can thrive in damp, crowded conditions.

Air circulation is particularly important in regions with high humidity. Planting your pomegranate trees too close together can create a microenvironment where moisture lingers on the leaves and fruit, encouraging the growth of mold and mildew. Proper spacing helps mitigate these risks and promotes healthier trees with better fruit quality.

In commercial orchards, high-density planting techniques can be used to maximize yield per acre. However, this approach requires more intensive management, including frequent pruning and careful attention to soil fertility and water management. For most home gardeners, standard spacing is more practical and ensures that each tree receives the care it needs to thrive.

When planning your pomegranate tree's layout, consider the mature size of the variety you are planting. Dwarf or compact varieties may require less space, while larger, more vigorous varieties will need more room to spread. Adjust your spacing accordingly to accommodate the specific growth habits of your chosen variety.

Companion Planting: Plants That Benefit Pomegranates

Companion planting is a gardening technique that involves growing different plants in close proximity to enhance growth, improve soil health, and reduce pest problems. When it comes to pomegranates, selecting the right companion plants can help boost the tree's overall health and productivity. Companion plants can attract beneficial insects, repel pests, and even provide natural mulch for your pomegranate tree.

Herbs such as basil, dill, and oregano are excellent companions for pomegranates. These aromatic plants attract pollinators, such as bees and butterflies, which help improve fruit set. At the same time, their strong scents can deter common garden pests, such as aphids and whiteflies, that may otherwise target your pomegranate tree. Growing these herbs around the base of your tree can create a natural defense system that benefits both the tree and the surrounding plants.

Planting Pomegranate with Companion Plants

Legumes, such as beans and peas, are another valuable addition to a pomegranate garden. These nitrogen-fixing plants help enrich the soil by converting atmospheric nitrogen into a form that plants can use. Growing legumes as a cover crop or interplanting them with your pomegranate tree can improve soil fertility, reducing the need for synthetic fertilizers. This natural boost in nutrients supports the healthy growth of your pomegranate tree throughout the growing season.

Flowering plants, such as marigolds and nasturtiums, are also beneficial companions for pomegranates. Marigolds release compounds into the soil that repel nematodes, tiny worms that can damage plant roots. Nasturtiums, on the other hand, attract aphids away from your pomegranate tree, serving as a "trap crop" that keeps pests from infesting the tree itself. These flowers also add beauty to your garden, making it a more pleasant space to spend time in.

Cover crops, such as clover and alfalfa, can be grown around pomegranate trees to improve soil structure and prevent erosion. These low-growing plants help retain moisture in the soil, reducing the need for frequent watering. As they decompose, cover crops also add organic matter to the soil, enhancing its ability to retain nutrients and support healthy root growth.

When selecting companion plants for your pomegranate tree, consider the specific needs of your garden. Choose plants that complement the growing conditions of your site, and arrange them in a way that maximizes their benefits to your pomegranate tree. Thoughtful companion planting can create a thriving garden ecosystem that supports healthy growth and reduces the need for chemical inputs.

Chapter 4

Caring for Young Pomegranate Trees

Young pomegranate trees require careful attention to ensure they establish themselves and grow into healthy, productive plants. While pomegranates are known for their resilience, the early stages of growth are crucial for setting the foundation for a successful tree. Proper watering, fertilizing, pest control, and structural support all play important roles in nurturing a thriving young pomegranate tree.

Watering Techniques: How Much and How Often

Watering Young Pomegranate Tree

Watering young pomegranate trees correctly is essential for healthy root development and overall growth. Unlike mature trees that can tolerate drought conditions, young pomegranates require consistent moisture to establish strong roots. Deep watering is the preferred method, as it encourages the roots to grow deeper into the soil, which makes the tree more resilient to dry periods as it matures.

During the first year after planting, water the tree deeply once or twice a week, depending on the weather and soil conditions. In hotter climates, more frequent watering may be necessary, especially during periods of extreme heat or drought. The goal is to keep the soil evenly moist but not waterlogged, as overly saturated soil can lead to root rot and other problems. Checking the moisture level in the soil by inserting your finger a few inches deep can help determine if watering is needed.

Drip irrigation systems are particularly effective for watering young pomegranate trees. These systems deliver water directly to the root zone, minimizing evaporation and ensuring that the water reaches where it's needed most. Mulching around the base of the tree can also help retain soil moisture and reduce the need for frequent watering. Organic mulches like straw, wood chips, or compost are ideal for this purpose, as they break down over time and enrich the soil.

As the tree matures and its root system expands, the frequency of watering can be reduced. Mature pomegranate trees are more drought-tolerant, but they still benefit from deep watering during the growing season, especially during flowering and fruit development. Ensuring that young trees receive adequate water during their first few years will lead to stronger, healthier plants capable of withstanding environmental stress.

Monitoring the tree's leaves can also provide clues about its watering needs. Drooping leaves may indicate that the tree is stressed from lack of water, while yellowing leaves can be a sign of overwatering. Adjusting your watering schedule based on the tree's response will help maintain the right balance of moisture in the soil.

Proper watering techniques are essential for establishing a strong foundation for young pomegranate trees. Providing consistent moisture, using efficient irrigation methods, and monitoring the tree's health will support vigorous growth and prepare the tree for future productivity.

Fertilizing for Healthy Growth

Fertilizing young pomegranate trees helps provide them with the essential nutrients they need for rapid growth and development. In the early stages of growth, pomegranates benefit from a balanced fertilizer that includes nitrogen, phosphorus, and potassium, as well as trace minerals like calcium, magnesium, and iron. These nutrients promote healthy root development, strong branches, and vibrant foliage.

Fertilizing should begin in the spring after planting and continue throughout the growing season. For young trees, applying a slow-release granular fertilizer is an effective way to provide a steady supply of nutrients over time. Avoid using high-nitrogen fertilizers, as they can lead to excessive vegetative growth at the expense of fruit production. Instead, choose a balanced fertilizer with an equal ratio of nitrogen, phosphorus, and potassium (NPK), such as a 10-10-10 or 12-12-12 blend.

In addition to granular fertilizers, incorporating organic matter into the soil can improve fertility and enhance the soil structure. Compost, aged manure, and worm castings are excellent sources of nutrients that also promote healthy soil biology. Organic amendments can be applied in the spring and fall to provide a boost of nutrients and help the tree transition through seasonal changes.

Fertilizer application should be timed to coincide with the tree's growth stages. In early spring, as the tree begins to break dormancy, an application of fertilizer helps kickstart growth. Additional applications can be made in late spring and early summer to support the tree during its most active growing period. Avoid fertilizing in late summer or fall, as this can encourage new growth that may not harden off before winter, leaving the tree vulnerable to cold damage.

Monitoring the tree's foliage can provide insights into its nutrient needs. Pale or yellow leaves may indicate a nitrogen deficiency, while stunted growth or poor fruit set can suggest a lack of phosphorus or potassium. Soil testing can also help identify specific nutrient deficiencies and guide your fertilization strategy.

Ensuring that young pomegranate trees receive the right balance of nutrients is crucial for their early development. By providing targeted fertilization throughout the growing season, you can promote healthy growth and prepare the tree for future fruit production.

Weed and Pest Control Strategies

Weeds and pests can pose significant challenges to young pomegranate trees, competing for resources and potentially harming the tree's health. Effective weed and pest control strategies are essential for protecting the tree and ensuring that it has the best possible start in its new environment. While pomegranates are relatively resistant to many pests, vigilance is key to preventing problems before they escalate.

Weed control begins with proper site preparation before planting. Removing existing weeds and applying a layer of mulch can help suppress new weed growth around the base of the tree. Organic mulches, such as straw or wood chips, not only reduce weed competition but also help retain soil moisture and improve soil structure over time. Applying mulch in a thick layer, at least 2 to 3 inches deep, is recommended for maximum weed suppression.

If weeds do emerge, hand-pulling is often the best method for controlling them around young trees. Avoid using herbicides, especially near the root zone, as they can harm the tree or disrupt beneficial soil organisms. Regular weeding throughout the growing season will help prevent weeds from establishing and competing with the tree for water and nutrients.

Pest control for young pomegranate trees focuses on preventing infestations before they become serious. Common pests that may affect pomegranates include aphids, scale insects, and mealybugs. These pests can weaken the tree by feeding on its sap and causing damage to the leaves, branches, and fruit. Regularly inspecting the tree for signs of pests, such as sticky residue, discolored leaves, or clusters of insects, can help you catch problems early.

Introducing beneficial insects, such as ladybugs and lacewings, can be an effective way to control pest populations naturally. These predators feed on harmful pests, reducing the need for chemical treatments. If pests become a significant issue, using organic insecticidal soaps or neem oil can help manage infestations without harming beneficial insects or the environment.

In some cases, physical barriers, such as tree guards or netting, can protect young pomegranate trees from larger pests like birds or rodents. These barriers prevent animals from feeding on the tree's leaves, fruit, or bark, which can be especially important during the early stages of growth.

Implementing a combination of weed and pest control strategies will help protect your young pomegranate tree and support its healthy development. Staying proactive and addressing issues as they arise will create a thriving environment for your tree to grow and flourish.

Training and Staking Your Tree

Training young pomegranate trees involves shaping them for structural strength and future productivity. Proper training helps create a balanced framework of branches that can support the weight of fruit and withstand wind and other environmental factors. While pomegranates can naturally take on a shrub-like form, training them as a small tree is a popular option for home gardeners and orchardists.

Training begins with selecting a central leader, which will become the main trunk of the tree. This central leader should be straight and strong, with evenly spaced branches growing outward from it. Pruning away any competing leaders or crossing branches will help establish a clear structure and prevent overcrowding. A well-spaced canopy allows sunlight to reach all parts of the tree, promoting even growth and fruit development.

Training and Staking Young Pomegranate Tree

Staking may be necessary during the first few years of growth to support the young tree and prevent it from being damaged by wind or heavy rain. A sturdy stake should be placed next to the tree, and soft ties should be used to secure the tree to the stake without constricting its growth. Ties should be checked regularly and adjusted as the tree grows to avoid damage to the trunk.

As the tree matures, lower branches can be pruned to create a clear trunk and encourage an open, vase-shaped canopy. This structure allows for better air circulation and easier access for pruning, harvesting, and maintenance. Regular pruning during the tree's early years will help guide its shape and ensure that it grows into a strong, productive plant.

In addition to structural training, young pomegranate trees may require thinning to reduce the number of fruiting branches. Overloaded branches can break under the weight of the fruit, so removing excess growth will help the remaining branches develop stronger fruit. Thinning also allows more light and air to reach the fruit, improving its quality and reducing the risk of disease.

Training and staking are critical components of caring for young pomegranate trees, helping to establish a strong, well-structured tree that can support abundant fruit production in the years to come.

Chapter 5

Pruning Techniques for Maximum Yield

Pruning is an essential practice for maintaining the health and productivity of pomegranate trees. While pomegranates are naturally vigorous growers, controlled pruning ensures that the tree develops a strong structure and produces high-quality fruit. Knowing the right timing and techniques for pruning is crucial for enhancing your tree's productivity and ensuring its overall health.

Understanding Pomegranate Growth Habits

Pruning Pomegranate to maintain tree health and productivity

Pomegranate trees are naturally bushy and can grow as multi-stemmed shrubs or be trained as single-trunk trees. Their vigorous growth habit allows them to produce an abundance of branches, which, if left unpruned, can lead to overcrowding and reduced fruit quality. Understanding how pomegranates grow is essential for determining the best approach to pruning and managing the tree's development.

Pomegranates produce fruit on new growth, typically from branches that are one year old. As such, pruning encourages the development of new shoots, which in turn increases the potential for fruit production. However, excessive pruning can reduce the overall yield, as it may remove too much of the tree's fruiting wood. Striking a balance between promoting new growth and preserving enough branches for fruiting is the goal of effective pruning.

The tree's natural growth pattern also means that it can develop multiple suckers from the base, which can compete with the main trunk for resources. Removing these suckers regularly helps maintain the tree's shape and directs energy toward fruit production rather than vegetative growth. Pruning also helps improve air circulation within the canopy, reducing the risk of fungal diseases and promoting overall tree health.

Pomegranate trees have a relatively long lifespan and can remain productive for many years with proper care. Regular pruning ensures that the tree continues to produce high-quality fruit while maintaining a manageable size and shape. Understanding the tree's growth habits allows gardeners to make informed decisions about how and when to prune for maximum benefit.

Recognizing the natural tendencies of pomegranate growth is the foundation of successful pruning. Tailoring your pruning approach to the tree's needs will result in a healthier, more productive plant that consistently delivers excellent fruit.

When and How to Prune

Timing is crucial when it comes to pruning pomegranate trees. The best time to prune is during the dormant season, typically in late winter or early spring, before new growth begins. Pruning during dormancy allows the tree to heal and recover before it enters its active growing phase. It also provides a clear view of the tree's structure, making it easier to identify which branches need to be removed or shaped.

When pruning, start by removing any dead, diseased, or damaged branches. These branches can weaken the tree and become entry points for pests and diseases. Cutting them back to healthy wood ensures that the tree can focus its energy on producing new growth and fruit. Use sharp, clean pruning tools to make clean cuts, and avoid leaving stubs, as these can become breeding grounds for disease.

Next, focus on thinning the canopy to improve air circulation and sunlight penetration. Removing crowded or crossing branches helps reduce the risk of fungal infections, which thrive in dark, humid conditions. Thinning also allows sunlight to reach all parts of the tree, promoting even growth and ripening of the fruit. Aim to create an open, vase-like structure with well-spaced branches that allow for optimal light and airflow.

For pomegranate trees trained as single-trunk specimens, prune away any suckers or water sprouts that emerge from the base of the tree or along the trunk. These shoots can divert energy away from fruit production and should be removed as soon as they appear. In multi-stemmed shrubs, thinning out weaker stems and focusing on a few strong, well-spaced trunks will help maintain a balanced structure.

While heavy pruning can reduce the tree's fruit production for a season, it is sometimes necessary to rejuvenate an overgrown or neglected tree. Rejuvenation pruning involves cutting back the tree more aggressively to encourage new growth and restore its shape. This approach should be done gradually over a few years to avoid stressing the tree.

Pruning at the right time and in the right way promotes healthy growth and ensures that the tree remains productive for years to come. Each pruning session should be tailored to the tree's specific needs, taking into account its age, health, and growth pattern.

Shaping Your Tree for Strength and Productivity

Shaping a pomegranate tree involves guiding its growth to create a strong framework that can support the weight of fruit and withstand environmental stress. Whether growing the tree as a single-trunk specimen or a multi-stemmed shrub, proper shaping ensures that the tree develops a balanced, open structure that promotes healthy growth and fruit production.

In the first few years after planting, focus on developing a strong central leader if you're training the tree as a single trunk. Prune away competing leaders and select 3 to 5 evenly spaced branches to form the primary scaffold. These branches will become the main structural support for the tree, so choosing branches that are well-angled and spaced is essential for creating a sturdy framework.

For multi-stemmed pomegranates, select the strongest, healthiest stems to serve as the main trunks, and remove any weaker or crossing stems. Maintaining an open center by pruning away inward-growing branches allows light and air to reach the interior of the tree, reducing the risk of disease and promoting even fruit ripening. Thinning out excess growth each year helps maintain the tree's shape and prevents overcrowding.

Shaping also involves training the tree to grow in a manageable size. While pomegranates can grow quite large if left unpruned, maintaining a height that allows for easy harvesting and maintenance is recommended. Regular pruning and thinning help control the tree's size and shape, making it easier to care for and more productive in the long run.

In regions prone to high winds or heavy rains, shaping the tree with a strong, open framework reduces the risk of branches breaking under pressure. Well-pruned trees are less likely to suffer damage during storms, as their balanced structure distributes weight evenly and allows air to move freely through the canopy.

Shaping pomegranate trees is a dynamic process that requires ongoing attention and adjustments as the tree grows. Regular pruning, thinning, and training help create a well-structured tree that can support abundant fruit production and withstand the challenges of its environment.

Common Pruning Mistakes to Avoid

While pruning is an essential part of pomegranate care, it is easy to make mistakes that can impact the tree's health and productivity. One common mistake is over-pruning, which removes too much of the tree's foliage and reduces its ability to produce energy through photosynthesis. Over-pruned trees may struggle to recover, leading to stunted growth and reduced fruit production. It is important to strike a balance between removing excess growth and preserving enough leaves to support the tree's overall health.

Another mistake is pruning at the wrong time of year. Pruning during the active growing season can stimulate new growth that may not have time to harden off before winter, leaving the tree vulnerable to frost damage. It can also lead to a loss of flowers and fruit, as the tree directs its energy toward regrowth rather than fruiting. Pruning during dormancy allows the tree to focus on healing and prepares it for vigorous growth in the spring.

Improper pruning techniques, such as making cuts too close to the trunk or leaving stubs, can create entry points for pests and diseases. Clean, angled cuts made just above a healthy bud or branch collar are essential for promoting proper healing. Using sharp, sanitized tools reduces the risk of spreading disease between trees and ensures that cuts are clean and precise.

Failing to thin out the canopy is another common mistake. A dense, overcrowded tree is more susceptible to fungal infections and pest infestations, as air cannot circulate freely through the branches. Regular thinning and removing crossing or competing branches helps maintain a healthy, open structure that reduces the risk of disease and improves fruit quality.

Neglecting to remove suckers and water sprouts can also lead to issues with the tree's structure and productivity. These fast-growing shoots divert energy away from fruit production and can create weak, spindly growth that is prone to breaking. Regularly inspecting the tree and removing unwanted shoots ensures that the tree remains focused on developing strong, productive branches.

Avoiding these common pruning mistakes helps promote the long-term health and productivity of your pomegranate tree. Thoughtful, well-timed pruning ensures that the tree grows into a strong, resilient plant capable of producing abundant fruit year after year.

Chapter 6

Protecting Your Pomegranates from Pests and Diseases

Pomegranates are relatively hardy plants, but they are not immune to the challenges posed by pests and diseases. A healthy tree requires careful monitoring, early detection, and the application of effective control measures. Prevention is essential for keeping your pomegranate trees healthy, allowing them to flourish and yield plentiful fruit.

Identifying Common Pests and Diseases

Several pests commonly affect pomegranate trees, and knowing how to identify them early is crucial for protecting your plants. Aphids, small pear-shaped insects, are frequent visitors to pomegranate trees. They feed on sap, weakening the tree and causing leaves to curl and turn yellow. Aphids also excrete honeydew, a sticky substance that attracts ants and promotes the growth of sooty mold, further harming the plant.

Mealybugs are another common pest, recognizable by their white, cotton-like appearance. These insects cluster around the base of leaves and stems, sucking sap and stunting the tree's growth. Left unchecked, mealybug infestations can cause serious damage, particularly to young trees. Scale insects, which appear as small, oval bumps on the bark and leaves, can also infest pomegranates, leading to reduced vigor and fruit production.

Pomegranate trees are susceptible to a variety of fungal diseases, with Alternaria fruit rot being one of the most problematic. This disease manifests as dark spots on the fruit, which eventually rot, making the fruit inedible. Alternaria thrives in warm, wet conditions and can spread quickly if not addressed. Leaf spot, another fungal issue, causes brown or black lesions on the leaves, weakening the tree and reducing its ability to photosynthesize.

Heart rot is a more severe disease that affects the internal structure of the fruit. It can be challenging to detect, as the fruit may appear healthy on the outside while rotting on the inside. This disease typically results from poor air circulation or overwatering, both of which create conditions that allow the fungus to thrive.

Being vigilant about identifying pests and diseases allows for timely intervention, preventing widespread damage to your pomegranate trees. Early detection ensures that you can take action before infestations or infections become severe, helping to protect your plants from long-term harm.

Organic and Chemical Control Methods

Controlling pests and diseases effectively requires a combination of organic and chemical methods, depending on the severity of the problem and your personal gardening philosophy. Organic methods are generally preferred for home gardeners looking to minimize the use of chemicals in their gardens, but chemical treatments can be necessary in some cases to prevent widespread damage.

Introducing beneficial insects is an excellent organic approach to managing pests. Ladybugs and lacewings are natural predators of aphids, scale, and mealybugs. Releasing these beneficial insects into your garden helps reduce pest populations without the need for chemical sprays. Companion planting with herbs like basil, dill, and marigolds can also repel pests and attract beneficial insects.

In cases where pests are more persistent, insecticidal soaps or neem oil can be effective organic solutions. Insecticidal soaps work by suffocating pests, making them a good choice for aphids, scale, and mealybugs. Neem oil disrupts the life cycle of pests and can help control fungal diseases as well. These organic treatments are safe for use on food crops and won't harm beneficial insects when used appropriately.

Chemical control methods may be necessary when pest populations become overwhelming or when diseases threaten the health of the tree. Synthetic insecticides and fungicides can provide quick relief from infestations or infections. However, it's essential to use these products carefully and according to label instructions to avoid harming beneficial insects, pollinators, or the surrounding environment.

Systemic insecticides, which are absorbed by the plant and kill pests as they feed, can be effective for persistent issues like scale. Fungicides are useful for managing fungal diseases such as Alternaria and leaf spot, particularly during wet weather. Regular applications during the growing season can prevent the spread of these diseases and protect the fruit.

Balancing organic and chemical control methods allows for a more sustainable approach to managing pests and diseases. Selecting the right treatment based on the severity of the problem helps ensure that your pomegranate trees remain healthy and productive without unnecessary chemical exposure.

Preventative Measures to Keep Your Tree Healthy

Prevention is always the best strategy when it comes to protecting your pomegranate trees from pests and diseases. A healthy tree is better equipped to resist infestations and infections, so the goal is to create an environment that supports vigorous growth. Several preventative measures can help maintain the health of your pomegranate trees and reduce the likelihood of problems.

Proper site selection is the first line of defense. Pomegranate trees thrive in well-drained soil with good air circulation. Planting trees too close together can create a microclimate that encourages the growth of fungi and makes it easier for pests to spread. Ensure that your trees have enough space to grow and that air can move freely through the canopy.

Pruning is another essential preventative measure. Regularly thinning the branches helps improve air circulation and sunlight penetration, reducing the conditions that promote fungal growth. Removing dead, damaged, or diseased wood also helps prevent the spread of pests and diseases. After pruning, always sanitize your tools to avoid transferring pathogens between plants.

Maintaining proper watering practices is critical for disease prevention. Overwatering can create the damp conditions that fungi need to thrive, leading to issues like root rot and fruit rot. Watering deeply but infrequently encourages healthy root development and reduces the risk of fungal diseases. Mulching around the base of the tree can help retain soil moisture while also preventing splashing water from spreading disease spores onto the leaves and fruit.

Feeding your tree with the right nutrients also contributes to its overall health. Balanced fertilization supports strong growth, which in turn makes the tree more resistant to pests and diseases. Soil testing can help you determine whether your tree needs additional nutrients, such as nitrogen, phosphorus, or potassium, to stay healthy.

Incorporating these preventative measures into your regular gardening routine creates an environment where your pomegranate tree can thrive. Healthy, well-maintained trees are less likely to suffer from pest and disease problems, ensuring a more bountiful harvest.

Seasonal Maintenance for Disease Prevention

Seasonal maintenance is a key component of disease prevention for pomegranate trees. Different seasons bring different challenges, and adjusting your care practices throughout the year helps keep your trees healthy and productive. Paying attention to the needs of your tree in each season reduces the likelihood of disease and promotes overall vitality.

In the spring, as the tree begins to break dormancy, it's essential to inspect for any signs of disease that may have taken hold over the winter. Prune away any dead or diseased wood and apply a fungicide if necessary to protect against springtime fungal infections. Spring is also the time to apply a balanced fertilizer to give the tree the nutrients it needs for healthy growth.

During the summer, monitor your tree for signs of pests and diseases, particularly during periods of high humidity or rainfall. Regular watering is crucial during the growing season, but avoid overwatering, which can lead to problems like fruit splitting or fungal infections. Applying mulch around the base of the tree helps retain soil moisture and keep the roots cool.

In the fall, after harvesting, continue to monitor the tree for signs of disease. Removing fallen leaves and fruit from around the base of the tree helps prevent the spread of pathogens that can overwinter in debris. Prune any remaining dead or diseased branches and apply a light layer of compost or organic matter to replenish the soil before the tree enters dormancy.

Winter is a time for the tree to rest, but it's also an opportunity to prepare for the coming growing season. Apply a dormant spray, such as horticultural oil, to protect the tree from overwintering pests and fungal spores. Winter is also a good time to inspect and clean your pruning tools, ensuring that they are ready for use in the spring.

Adapting your care practices to the changing seasons is essential for preventing diseases and promoting the long-term health of your pomegranate tree. Seasonal maintenance tasks, from pruning in the spring to applying dormant sprays in the winter, help create an environment where your tree can thrive.

Chapter 7

Irrigation and Water Management

Effective irrigation and water management are critical to the success of your pomegranate tree. While pomegranates are drought-tolerant once established, they still require consistent moisture, especially during their early growth stages and fruiting period.

Setting Up an Efficient Irrigation System

An efficient irrigation system is one of the most valuable tools for maintaining healthy pomegranate trees. Drip irrigation is widely regarded as the best option for pomegranates, as it delivers water directly to the root zone, minimizing evaporation and ensuring that water reaches where it's needed most. Setting up a drip system is relatively simple and can be customized to suit the specific needs of your garden.

When designing your drip irrigation system, ensure that the emitters are spaced evenly around the tree's root zone. Typically, two to four emitters per tree are sufficient, depending on the size of the tree and the climate. Adjustable emitters allow you to control the flow rate, ensuring that each tree receives the right amount of water. In sandy soils, where water drains quickly, a slower flow rate may be beneficial, while in heavier soils, a faster flow can prevent water from pooling.

In regions with varying seasonal rainfall, installing a timer on your drip irrigation system helps regulate watering schedules. Timers can be programmed to water during the early morning hours, reducing water loss through evaporation and giving the soil time to absorb the moisture before the heat of the day. For more advanced systems, moisture sensors can be added to adjust watering frequency based on the soil's current moisture level.

Filters are an important component of drip irrigation systems, as they prevent clogs that can reduce the efficiency of the system. Regularly checking and cleaning the filters ensures that water flows smoothly and evenly to each tree. Additionally, consider using pressure regulators to maintain a consistent water flow, especially if you have multiple trees on the same line.

An efficient irrigation system is an investment in the long-term health of your pomegranate trees. By delivering water directly to the roots and minimizing waste, drip irrigation helps ensure that your trees receive the moisture they need to thrive, even in regions with limited rainfall.

The Importance of Mulching

Mulching plays a crucial role in conserving moisture and maintaining the health of your pomegranate tree. A thick layer of mulch around the base of the tree helps regulate soil temperature, reduces water evaporation, and prevents weed growth. Organic mulches, such as wood chips, straw, or compost, are particularly beneficial, as they gradually break down and enrich the soil with nutrients.

When applying mulch, spread it evenly in a circle around the tree, extending out to the drip line. The mulch layer should be 2 to 3 inches deep, thick enough to provide insulation and moisture retention, but not so thick that it smothers the roots. Avoid piling mulch directly against the trunk, as this can create conditions that encourage rot and pest infestations.

In addition to conserving moisture, mulch acts as a natural barrier against weeds, which can compete with the tree for water and nutrients. Mulching reduces the need for frequent weeding, saving time and effort while ensuring that the tree receives the resources it needs. As the mulch breaks down, it also improves soil structure, enhancing its ability to retain water and support healthy root development.

In hot climates, mulch helps keep the soil cool, protecting the roots from extreme temperatures. During the winter months, it insulates the soil, protecting the roots from frost damage. Mulching is a year-round practice that supports the tree's health through all seasons, making it an essential component of water management and overall care.

Dealing with Drought Conditions

Pomegranates are known for their drought tolerance, but even these resilient trees can suffer during extended periods of drought. Proper water management becomes even more critical during dry spells to ensure that your tree remains healthy and productive. When dealing with drought conditions, conserving water while still providing the tree with enough moisture is a delicate balance.

Deep, infrequent watering is the key to helping pomegranate trees survive drought. Shallow watering encourages roots to stay near the soil surface, where they are more susceptible to drying out. Instead, water deeply to encourage the roots to grow deeper into the soil, where they can access moisture that remains even during dry periods. This deep watering should be done once every two to three weeks, depending on the severity of the drought.

Mulching around the base of the tree becomes even more important during drought conditions, as it helps retain whatever moisture is available in the soil. A thick layer of mulch reduces evaporation and keeps the soil cooler, providing a more stable environment for the roots. If possible, use organic materials that break down slowly, providing long-lasting benefits to the soil.

In extreme drought conditions, reducing the tree's water needs through selective pruning can help it survive. Thinning out some of the foliage reduces the tree's demand for water, allowing it to conserve resources. However, be cautious not to over-prune, as this can stress the tree further.

During drought, it may also be necessary to prioritize which trees receive water. Mature pomegranate trees are more drought-tolerant than young trees, so focus on providing consistent moisture to younger, more vulnerable plants. If water restrictions are in place, consider using greywater or rainwater collected in barrels to supplement your irrigation efforts.

Signs of Overwatering and Underwatering

Overwatering and underwatering are two of the most common problems that pomegranate growers face, and recognizing the signs of both is crucial for maintaining a healthy tree. While pomegranates are relatively drought-tolerant, they still need a balanced watering routine to thrive. Too little water can stress the tree, while too much can lead to root rot and other serious issues.

Signs of underwatering are usually more straightforward to identify. The tree may show signs of wilting, with leaves drooping or curling inward. The leaves may also become dry and brittle, and in extreme cases, they may turn brown and drop prematurely. Fruit production may be affected, with smaller, less flavorful fruit being a common result of prolonged underwatering. The soil around the tree will feel dry to the touch, and cracks may appear on the surface.

Overwatering, on the other hand, can be more insidious. Symptoms of overwatering often resemble those of underwatering, making it easy to misdiagnose the problem. Yellowing leaves are a common sign of overwatering, as the roots begin to suffocate from excess moisture and fail to deliver nutrients to the rest of the tree. Root rot, caused by fungal pathogens that thrive in waterlogged soil, can also develop, leading to a decline in overall tree health.

The key to distinguishing between overwatering and underwatering lies in monitoring the soil. Checking the moisture level a few inches below the surface can provide insight into whether the tree is receiving too much or too little water. If the soil is consistently wet and the tree shows signs of stress, overwatering is likely the issue. If the soil is dry and crumbly, underwatering is the more probable cause.

Adjusting your watering practices based on the tree's response will help prevent these problems from worsening. If underwatering is the issue, increasing the frequency or duration of watering sessions can help the tree recover. For overwatered trees, reducing the amount of water and improving soil drainage are essential steps to allow the roots to breathe and recover.

Recognizing the signs of overwatering and underwatering early on can prevent long-term damage to your pomegranate tree. By closely monitoring soil moisture levels and adjusting your irrigation practices as needed, you can ensure that your tree receives the right amount of water for healthy growth.

Chapter 8

Fertilizing Your Pomegranate Tree

Fertilizing is a crucial aspect of caring for pomegranate trees, providing them with the nutrients they need to grow strong and produce high-quality fruit. From selecting the right type of fertilizer to understanding when and how to apply it, proper fertilization can significantly impact the health and productivity of your tree. Exploring the best practices for fertilizing will ensure that your pomegranate tree thrives in any growing environment.

Types of Fertilizers and Their Benefits

Fertilizers come in various forms, each offering unique benefits to pomegranate trees. The primary nutrients that pomegranates need are nitrogen (N), phosphorus (P), and potassium (K), often referred to as NPK. These macronutrients support different aspects of the tree's growth: nitrogen promotes healthy foliage, phosphorus encourages root development and flower production, and potassium enhances fruit quality and overall resilience.

Balanced fertilizers with an equal ratio of NPK, such as 10-10-10 or 12-12-12, are commonly used for pomegranate trees, as they provide a well-rounded nutrient profile. These fertilizers are suitable for promoting both vegetative growth and fruit production. However, depending on the soil and tree's specific needs, fertilizers with a higher concentration of one nutrient may be more appropriate. For example, a fertilizer with a higher phosphorus content can be beneficial during the flowering and fruiting stages, while nitrogen-rich fertilizers are ideal for early growth.

Compost can be used as an organic fertilizer for young pomegranate trees

Organic fertilizers, such as compost, aged manure, and bone meal, are popular choices for gardeners looking to enrich the soil naturally. These fertilizers not only provide essential nutrients but also improve soil structure and support beneficial soil organisms. Organic fertilizers release nutrients slowly over time, providing a steady supply to the tree without the risk of over-fertilization.

Liquid fertilizers, often used in foliar feeding, deliver nutrients directly to the leaves, allowing for quick absorption. This method can be particularly effective during the growing season when the tree requires an immediate nutrient boost. Liquid fertilizers can be used in conjunction with granular fertilizers to ensure that the tree receives a balanced diet throughout the year.

Specialized fertilizers designed specifically for fruit trees may also contain micronutrients such as calcium, magnesium, and zinc, which are important for overall tree health. These micronutrients support functions like cell wall development, chlorophyll production, and enzyme activation. Ensuring that your pomegranate tree receives a full spectrum of nutrients promotes vigorous growth and high-quality fruit.

Selecting the right type of fertilizer depends on your tree's growth stage, soil condition, and desired outcomes. Whether using organic or synthetic options, understanding the benefits of each type allows you to make informed decisions that support the long-term health of your pomegranate tree.

Homemade vs. Commercial Fertilizers

Both homemade and commercial fertilizers offer advantages when it comes to feeding pomegranate trees, and the choice between the two often depends on personal preferences, availability, and specific gardening goals. Homemade fertilizers are a great option for gardeners looking to recycle organic materials and create nutrient-rich blends tailored to their soil's needs. On the other hand, commercial fertilizers provide convenience and consistency, offering pre-mixed formulations designed for specific purposes.

Homemade fertilizers can be created using a variety of natural ingredients, such as kitchen scraps, compost, and manure. For example, banana peels are rich in potassium, making them an excellent addition to compost or as a direct mulch around the tree. Coffee grounds provide nitrogen, while eggshells contribute calcium. Creating a compost pile that includes a mix of green (nitrogen-rich) and brown (carbon-rich) materials can produce a well-balanced fertilizer that improves soil fertility and texture.

Another homemade option is compost tea, which is made by steeping compost in water for several days. This liquid fertilizer can be applied directly to the soil or used as a foliar spray, delivering nutrients in a readily accessible form. Compost tea not only feeds the tree but also introduces beneficial microorganisms that help break down organic matter and improve soil health.

Commercial fertilizers, on the other hand, are formulated to provide precise nutrient ratios based on the tree's needs. They are available in various forms, including granular, liquid, and slow-release pellets. One of the main advantages of commercial fertilizers is their consistency; each application delivers the exact amount of nutrients as indicated on the label. This predictability is especially helpful for gardeners who want to follow a specific fertilization schedule without the guesswork involved in homemade mixes.

For gardeners who prefer organic methods but want the convenience of commercial products, organic fertilizers are also widely available. These products are often made from plant, animal, or mineral sources and are designed to provide a slow, steady release of nutrients. Organic commercial fertilizers are ideal for gardeners looking to combine the benefits of natural materials with the ease of store-bought products.

Choosing between homemade and commercial fertilizers ultimately depends on your gardening style and goals. Both options can be effective, and many gardeners find that a combination of the two works best for their pomegranate trees. Understanding the pros and cons of each approach allows for a more tailored fertilization strategy that meets the needs of your specific garden.

Signs of Nutrient Deficiencies

Recognizing the signs of nutrient deficiencies in pomegranate trees is essential for ensuring that your tree receives the right balance of nutrients throughout the growing season. Deficiencies can manifest in various ways, often affecting the tree's foliage, growth rate, and fruit quality. Being able to diagnose these issues early allows for timely intervention and correction, helping to restore the tree's health and productivity.

Nitrogen deficiency is one of the most common nutrient issues in pomegranate trees, often presenting as pale or yellowing leaves. Nitrogen is essential for producing chlorophyll, the pigment responsible for photosynthesis. When the tree lacks nitrogen, its ability to produce energy is compromised, leading to stunted growth and reduced vigor. Addressing this deficiency with a nitrogen-rich fertilizer can help restore the tree's green, healthy foliage.

Phosphorus deficiency may be less visible but can significantly impact the tree's root development and fruit production. Symptoms include dark or purplish leaves, poor flowering, and reduced fruit set. Phosphorus is critical for energy transfer within the plant, so a lack of this nutrient can limit the tree's ability to grow and reproduce. Applying a phosphorus-rich fertilizer, such as bone meal or superphosphate, can help correct this deficiency and improve overall growth.

Potassium deficiency often manifests as brown or scorched leaf edges, as well as weak stems and poor fruit quality. Potassium plays a vital role in water regulation and enzyme activation, making it essential for overall tree health. Without enough potassium, the tree may struggle to transport water and nutrients, leading to wilting and reduced resistance to environmental stress. Potassium-rich fertilizers, such as potassium sulfate or wood ash, can help address this issue.

Micronutrient deficiencies, such as a lack of calcium, magnesium, or iron, can also affect pomegranate trees. Calcium deficiency often presents as distorted or brittle new growth, while magnesium deficiency causes yellowing between the veins of older leaves. Iron deficiency, known as chlorosis, results in yellowing leaves with green veins, particularly in young growth. Addressing these deficiencies requires the application of specific micronutrient supplements or soil amendments.

Monitoring your tree regularly for signs of nutrient deficiencies allows for early intervention and correction. Ensuring that the tree receives a balanced diet of macro and micronutrients promotes healthy growth and helps prevent long-term damage.

Fertilization Schedule for Different Seasons

Creating a fertilization schedule that aligns with the pomegranate tree's growth cycle is key to providing the right nutrients at the right time. Seasonal adjustments in fertilization ensure that the tree receives what it needs to thrive during different stages of its development, from initial growth to fruiting and dormancy.

In early spring, as the tree begins to break dormancy, it's time to apply the first round of fertilizer. This initial application should focus on promoting new growth, so a balanced fertilizer with equal parts nitrogen, phosphorus, and potassium is ideal. Organic fertilizers, such as compost or manure, can also be applied at this time to enrich the soil and support healthy root development. The goal is to provide the tree with the energy it needs to start the growing season strong.

As the tree moves into late spring and early summer, a second application of fertilizer helps sustain its growth and encourages flowering. During this period, pomegranate trees benefit from a phosphorus-rich fertilizer that supports flower and fruit development. Liquid fertilizers can also be used as a supplement, providing an additional boost during the critical fruit-setting phase. Ensuring that the tree has enough nutrients at this stage helps maximize fruit production and quality.

In mid to late summer, as the fruit begins to develop, a potassium-rich fertilizer can be applied to enhance fruit size, flavor, and resilience. Potassium is particularly important during the fruiting stage, as it helps regulate water balance and improves the tree's ability to transport nutrients to the developing fruit. Applying a slow-release potassium fertilizer ensures that the tree continues to receive this vital nutrient throughout the fruiting period.

As fall approaches and the tree begins to prepare for dormancy, it's time to reduce or stop fertilization altogether. Fertilizing too late in the season can encourage new growth that may not have time to harden off before winter, leaving the tree vulnerable to cold damage. Instead, focus on maintaining soil health with a light layer of compost or mulch to protect the roots during the winter months.

Following a seasonal fertilization schedule tailored to the tree's growth stages ensures that your pomegranate tree receives the nutrients it needs to thrive. Adjusting the type and timing of fertilizers throughout the year helps support healthy growth, abundant fruit production, and overall tree vitality.

Chapter 9

Harvesting Pomegranates: Timing and Techniques

Harvesting pomegranates at the right time and using proper techniques are crucial for ensuring that the fruit reaches its full potential in flavor, texture, and shelf life. Knowing when and how to harvest, as well as how to handle and store the fruit afterward can make all the difference in the quality of your pomegranate harvest.

When Is the Right Time to Harvest?

Harvesting ripe pomegranates

Determining the right time to harvest pomegranates can be challenging, as the fruit does not continue to ripen after being picked. The key is to harvest when the fruit has reached its peak maturity, which typically occurs in late summer to early fall, depending on your climate and variety. Pomegranates are ready for harvest when they have developed their characteristic deep color and sound hollow when tapped.

The appearance of the fruit is one of the best indicators of ripeness. The skin should be smooth and firm, with no green coloration remaining. The color of the skin can vary depending on the variety, ranging from deep red to pink or even yellow. However, the intensity of the color, rather than the specific hue, is a good indicator of ripeness. The fruit should also feel heavy for its size, indicating that it is full of juice.

In addition to visual cues, the shape of the fruit can also signal readiness for harvest. Ripe pomegranates often take on a slightly flattened or hexagonal shape, as the arils inside swell and push against the skin. The calyx, or crown, at the top of the fruit may begin to open slightly, indicating that the fruit is fully mature.

Weather conditions can also influence the timing of the harvest. If a period of heavy rain is expected, it's best to harvest the fruit beforehand to avoid water damage or splitting. Similarly, in regions prone to early frosts, harvesting before the first frost is essential to prevent the fruit from freezing on the tree.

Knowing when to harvest requires careful observation and experience. Monitoring the fruit closely as it approaches maturity and using a combination of visual, tactile, and environmental cues helps ensure that you pick your pomegranates at the perfect time.

How to Harvest Without Damaging the Fruit

Proper harvesting techniques are essential for preventing damage to the pomegranate fruit, which can reduce its quality and shelf life. Unlike some other fruits, pomegranates should not be pulled or twisted from the tree, as this can tear the skin or break the stem too close to the fruit, leading to early spoilage. Instead, using sharp pruning shears or a knife is the best method for harvesting pomegranates safely.

When harvesting, cut the stem about an inch above the fruit, leaving a short length of stem attached. This minimizes the risk of damage to the skin and helps protect the fruit during handling and storage. Be gentle when placing the fruit in a container, as pomegranates can bruise easily if dropped or stacked too high. Using padded or lined baskets can help prevent bruising, especially if harvesting large quantities of fruit.

It's also important to avoid harvesting during the hottest part of the day, as the fruit can become more sensitive to bruising when it's warm. Early morning or late afternoon is the ideal time for harvesting, as the fruit is cooler and less prone to damage. If possible, harvest on a dry day to reduce the risk of introducing moisture into the storage area, which can promote mold growth.

For larger harvests, consider using a picking tool or pole with a cutting attachment to reach higher branches without damaging the tree or fruit. This method allows you to access the upper parts of the tree without the need for ladders, reducing the risk of injury and making the process more efficient.

Ensuring that your harvesting techniques are gentle and precise helps preserve the quality of the fruit and extends its shelf life. Taking the time to harvest carefully can make a significant difference in the enjoyment of your pomegranate crop.

Post-Harvest Handling and Storage Tips

Once the pomegranates are harvested, proper handling and storage are crucial for maintaining their freshness and flavor. Pomegranates have a relatively long shelf life compared to many other fruits, but they still require the right conditions to remain at their best. Post-harvest handling begins with sorting the fruit and removing any damaged or bruised pomegranates, as these are more prone to spoilage.

Pomegranates should be stored in a cool, dry place with good air circulation. Ideal storage temperatures range from 40°F to 50°F (4°C to 10°C), which helps slow down the ripening process and extend the fruit's shelf life. Under these conditions, pomegranates can last for several weeks to a few months. If you have a large harvest, consider storing the fruit in a refrigerator or a cool cellar to maintain optimal conditions.

It's important to avoid storing pomegranates in plastic bags or airtight containers, as this can trap moisture and promote mold growth. Instead, store the fruit in a well-ventilated container, such as a mesh bag or a wooden crate, that allows air to circulate freely. If storing in a refrigerator, keep the pomegranates in the crisper drawer or on a shelf where they won't be exposed to excess humidity.

If you plan to store pomegranate arils (seeds) separately, they can be removed from the fruit and stored in an airtight container in the refrigerator for up to a week. For longer storage, the arils can be frozen. To freeze, spread the arils in a single layer on a baking sheet and freeze until solid, then transfer them to a freezer-safe container or bag. Frozen arils can last for several months and are perfect for adding to smoothies, salads, or desserts.

Proper post-harvest handling and storage ensure that your pomegranates retain their flavor, texture, and nutritional value for as long as possible. Creating the right storage conditions helps you enjoy the fruits of your labor well into the fall and winter months.

Preparing Your Tree for the Next Season

After harvesting, preparing your pomegranate tree for the next growing season is essential for ensuring continued health and productivity. Post-harvest care involves a combination of pruning, fertilizing, and general maintenance to help the tree recover from the fruiting season and enter dormancy in a strong, healthy state.

Pruning is one of the most important tasks after harvesting. Removing any dead, damaged, or diseased branches helps improve air circulation and reduces the risk of pests and diseases overwintering in the tree. Thinning out crowded branches also encourages new growth in the spring and improves fruit production for the next season. For trees that have grown too large, light pruning can help control their size and shape without over-stressing the tree.

Post-harvest fertilization is another key component of preparing the tree for the next season. Applying a light layer of compost or organic fertilizer in the fall helps replenish the nutrients that the tree used during the fruiting period. However, avoid heavy fertilization at this time, as it can encourage new growth that may not have time to harden off before winter. The goal is to support the tree's natural recovery process without overstimulating growth.

Mulching around the base of the tree helps protect the roots from cold temperatures and maintains soil moisture throughout the winter. Organic mulches, such as straw or wood chips, also break down over time, adding nutrients to the soil and improving its structure. Applying mulch in the fall creates a protective barrier that insulates the roots and supports healthy growth in the spring.

Inspecting the tree for pests and diseases before winter sets in is another essential task. Removing any remaining fruit, fallen leaves, or debris from around the tree reduces the risk of pests and pathogens overwintering in the soil or on the tree itself. Applying a dormant oil spray can help protect the tree from overwintering insects, such as scale or mites, by suffocating their eggs and larvae.

Chapter 10

Preserving Pomegranates: Beyond Fresh Consumption

Pomegranates are prized for their vibrant, juicy seeds and sweet-tart flavor, but their shelf life can be limited when kept fresh. Fortunately, there are numerous ways to preserve pomegranates, allowing you to enjoy their unique taste and health benefits long after the harvest season has ended. From freezing and canning to creating delicious syrups and dried arils, these preservation techniques ensure that pomegranates remain a staple in your kitchen throughout the year.

Freezing and Canning Techniques

Freezing is one of the simplest and most effective methods for preserving pomegranates, especially the arils (seeds). To freeze pomegranate arils, start by carefully removing them from the fruit. Spread the arils in a single layer on a baking sheet lined with parchment paper, ensuring they are not touching each other. This step prevents them from clumping together during freezing. Place the baking sheet in the freezer for a few hours until the arils are completely frozen. Once frozen, transfer them to airtight containers or freezer bags, where they can be stored for up to six months. Frozen arils are perfect for adding to smoothies, salads, or desserts, retaining their flavor and nutritional value.

Canning pomegranate juice or syrup is another excellent way to preserve the fruit's essence. Begin by juicing the pomegranates, either by hand or using a juicer. For juice, simply pour the liquid into sterilized canning jars, leaving about half an inch of headspace. Process the jars in a water bath canner for about 15 minutes to ensure they are properly sealed. The juice can be stored in a cool, dark place for up to a year. For syrup, simmer the pomegranate juice with sugar until it thickens to the desired consistency. Pour the hot syrup into sterilized jars and process them in the same way as the juice. Pomegranate syrup can be used in cocktails, drizzled over pancakes, or added to marinades for a burst of flavor.

Canned pomegranate arils are another option, though they require a bit more preparation. Start by blanching the arils in boiling water for a few minutes to soften them slightly. Pack the blanched arils into sterilized jars, then cover them with a light syrup made from sugar and water. Process the jars in a water bath canner to seal them. Canned arils can be used in recipes where a softer texture is desirable, such as in sauces or baked goods.

These freezing and canning techniques allow you to enjoy the taste and health benefits of pomegranates throughout the year, even when fresh fruit is not in season. The versatility of frozen and canned pomegranates makes them a valuable addition to any kitchen, ready to enhance a wide range of dishes.

Making Pomegranate Juice and Syrup

Pomegranate juice and syrup are versatile ingredients that capture the fruit's vibrant flavor and can be used in a variety of culinary applications. Making pomegranate juice at home is straightforward and yields a fresh, pure product free from additives. To make the juice, start by cutting the pomegranates in half and extracting the seeds. You can juice the seeds using a hand-held citrus juicer, a countertop juicer, or even by pressing them through a fine-mesh strainer with the back of a spoon. The result is a richly colored juice with a balanced sweet-tart flavor that can be enjoyed on its own or used as a base for other beverages.

Homemade Pomegranate Juice

Pomegranate syrup, or grenadine, is made by reducing pomegranate juice with sugar until it reaches a thick, pourable consistency. This syrup is a key ingredient in many classic cocktails, such as the tequila sunrise, but it can also be drizzled over desserts, stirred into yogurt, or used as a glaze for meats. To make the syrup, combine equal parts pomegranate juice and sugar in a saucepan. Heat the mixture over medium heat, stirring until the sugar is completely dissolved. Reduce the heat to low and simmer the mixture until it thickens to your desired consistency, which usually takes about 30 to 45 minutes. For added depth of flavor, consider adding a splash of lemon juice or a pinch of salt.

Another way to enhance the flavor of pomegranate syrup is by infusing it with spices. Adding cinnamon sticks, cloves, or vanilla pods during the simmering process can create a syrup with warm, aromatic notes, perfect for holiday recipes. Once the syrup has thickened, remove the spices and pour the syrup into sterilized jars. Store the jars in the refrigerator, where the syrup will keep for several months.

Both pomegranate juice and syrup can be incorporated into a wide range of recipes. Use the juice as a base for smoothies, cocktails, or mocktails, or freeze it in ice cube trays for a refreshing addition to sparkling water. The syrup can be used to sweeten and flavor everything from breakfast dishes to savory marinades, offering a concentrated taste of pomegranate that elevates any dish.

Making pomegranate juice and syrup at home allows you to control the ingredients and ensure a fresh, high-quality product. These homemade versions capture the essence of pomegranate and bring its unique flavor to a variety of culinary creations.

Drying Pomegranate Seeds (Arils)

Drying pomegranate seeds, or arils, is a fantastic way to preserve their flavor and nutritional value in a shelf-stable form. Dried pomegranate arils can be used as a crunchy topping for salads, added to trail mix, or incorporated into baked goods, providing a burst of sweet-tart flavor and a pleasing texture. The process of drying arils is relatively simple and can be done using a dehydrator, an oven, or even air drying in certain climates.

To begin drying pomegranate arils, start by removing the seeds from the fruit and spreading them in a single layer on a dehydrator tray or a baking sheet lined with parchment paper. If using a dehydrator, set the temperature to 135°F (57°C) and dry the arils for about 12 to 18 hours, or until they are completely dry and crisp. If using an oven, set it to the lowest possible temperature, ideally around 150°F (65°C), and dry the arils for 10 to 12 hours. Keep the oven door slightly ajar to allow moisture to escape. Stirring the arils occasionally during drying helps ensure they dry evenly.

Air drying is an option in climates with low humidity. Spread the arils on a mesh screen or a tray covered with cheesecloth and place them in a well-ventilated area out of direct sunlight. This method may take several days, depending on the humidity and temperature, but it's a low-energy way to preserve pomegranates.

Once the arils are fully dried, store them in an airtight container in a cool, dark place. Properly dried and stored arils can last for up to a year. Dried pomegranate arils are a convenient snack on their own, or they can be rehydrated by soaking them in water or juice for a few hours before use in recipes.

Dried pomegranate arils add a unique texture and flavor to both sweet and savory dishes. Sprinkle them over oatmeal, yogurt, or salads for a nutritious boost, or mix them into granola and energy bars. Their concentrated flavor and versatility make them a valuable addition to your pantry, ready to enhance a variety of meals.

Drying pomegranate seeds is an effective way to extend the fruit's shelf life while preserving its vibrant flavor and health benefits. This simple preservation method provides a convenient way to enjoy the taste of pomegranates long after the fresh fruit is gone.

Innovative Recipes Using Preserved Pomegranates

Pomegranate Glazed Roasted Vegetables

Preserved pomegranates, whether frozen, dried, or turned into syrup, offer a world of culinary possibilities beyond simple snacking. These preserved forms can be used to create innovative dishes that highlight the fruit's unique flavor profile, adding a touch of sophistication to both everyday meals and special occasions. Exploring creative ways to use preserved pomegranates can elevate your cooking and introduce exciting new flavors to your repertoire.

One innovative recipe is pomegranate-glazed roasted vegetables. In this dish, a mixture of pomegranate syrup, olive oil, and balsamic vinegar is brushed over root vegetables such as carrots, sweet potatoes, and parsnips before roasting. The syrup caramelizes in the oven, adding a rich, tangy sweetness that complements the earthy flavors of the vegetables. This dish makes an impressive side for holiday meals or can be served as a vegetarian main course.

Pomegranate arils can also be used to create a unique twist on traditional pesto. Instead of the usual pine nuts, try using dried pomegranate seeds as the base. Blend the arils with fresh basil, garlic, Parmesan cheese, and olive oil to create a vibrant, tangy pesto that pairs beautifully with pasta, grilled meats, or as a spread on sandwiches. The dried arils add a crunchy texture and a burst of flavor that sets this pesto apart from the classic version.

For dessert, consider making pomegranate and dark chocolate truffles. These rich, indulgent treats are made by mixing dried pomegranate arils with melted dark chocolate, then rolling the mixture into small balls and coating them with cocoa powder. The tartness of the pomegranate contrasts beautifully with the bittersweet chocolate, creating a sophisticated flavor combination that is sure to impress. These truffles make an elegant gift or a luxurious after-dinner treat.

Preserved pomegranate syrup can also be used to create a flavorful marinade for meats. Combine the syrup with soy sauce, garlic, ginger, and a splash of rice vinegar to create a tangy-sweet marinade for chicken, pork, or beef. The syrup not only adds flavor but also helps tenderize the meat, resulting in a juicy, flavorful dish. This marinade is especially well-suited for grilling, as the sugars in the syrup caramelize on the grill, adding depth and complexity to the dish.

Innovative recipes using preserved pomegranates allow you to explore new culinary horizons and make the most of your preserved harvest. From savory dishes to sweet treats, preserved pomegranates add a unique twist to a wide range of recipes, bringing the taste of this vibrant fruit to your table year-round.

Chapter 11

Propagating Pomegranate Trees

Pomegranate trees can be propagated using a variety of methods, including seeds, cuttings, and grafting. Each method has its own advantages and challenges, and the choice of propagation technique depends on factors such as the desired characteristics of the tree, available resources, and personal preference. Understanding the different methods of propagation can help you successfully grow new pomegranate trees that are healthy and productive.

Methods of Propagation: Seeds, Cuttings, and Grafting

Growing pomegranate trees from seeds is one of the simplest and most accessible methods of propagation, though it requires patience and a bit of luck. Pomegranate seeds can be collected from ripe fruit and planted in well-draining soil. It's important to clean the seeds thoroughly to remove any remaining pulp, which can inhibit germination. Plant the seeds about half an inch deep and keep the soil consistently moist but not waterlogged. Germination can take several weeks to a few months, depending on the conditions.

While growing pomegranates from seeds is relatively easy, it's important to note that seed-grown trees may not produce fruit that is identical to the parent plant. Pomegranates are often cross-pollinated, meaning the seeds may carry traits from different varieties. This can result in trees with fruit that is different in flavor, size, or quality from the original. For this reason, seed propagation is often used for experimentation or as a fun project rather than for producing consistent, high-quality fruit.

Propagation by cuttings is a more reliable method for producing pomegranate trees that are true to the parent plant. Hardwood cuttings taken from mature branches are the most commonly used for this method. Choose a healthy branch that is about a pencil's thickness and 8 to 10 inches long. Remove any leaves from the lower part of the cutting and dip the cut end in rooting hormone to encourage root development. Plant the cutting in a well-draining potting mix, keeping it moist and in a warm location. Over the next few months, the cutting should develop roots and begin to grow into a new tree.

Grafting is another method of propagating pomegranate trees, though it requires more skill and experience. Grafting involves joining a scion, or a piece of a desired variety, to the rootstock of another tree. This method is often used to combine the hardiness or disease resistance of one tree with the fruiting qualities of another. Grafting is particularly useful for creating dwarf or multi-variety trees, where different types of pomegranates can be grown on the same rootstock. Proper care and precision are essential for successful grafting, as the union between the scion and rootstock must be secure and well-aligned.

Each method of propagation offers unique advantages, allowing growers to select the best approach based on their goals and resources. Whether growing from seeds, cuttings, or grafting, propagating pomegranate trees is a rewarding process that can result in healthy, productive trees for years to come.

Step-by-Step Guide to Successful Propagation

Propagating pomegranate trees requires careful attention to detail at every stage of the process, from selecting the right materials to providing the proper care as the new plants develop. By following a step-by-step approach, you can increase your chances of success and grow strong, healthy trees.

For seed propagation, start by selecting ripe pomegranates and extracting the seeds. Clean the seeds thoroughly and allow them to dry for a few days before planting. Use a seed-starting mix in small pots or seed trays, and plant the seeds about half an inch deep. Keep the soil consistently moist and place the pots in a warm, bright location, such as a sunny windowsill or a greenhouse. Germination can take several weeks, so be patient and keep an eye on the moisture levels to prevent the seeds from drying out.

If you're propagating by cuttings, choose healthy branches from a mature pomegranate tree. Cuttings should be taken during the tree's dormant season, typically in late winter. Prepare the cuttings by removing any leaves from the lower part and dipping the cut end in rooting hormone. Plant the cuttings in a well-draining potting mix, and keep the soil consistently moist. Place the cuttings in a warm location with indirect sunlight. Over time, the cuttings will develop roots and begin to grow.

For grafting, select a healthy scion from a pomegranate variety with desirable fruit qualities and a compatible rootstock. Grafting is best done during the dormant season when the tree is not actively growing. Make clean cuts on both the scion and the rootstock, ensuring that the cambium layers (the green, growing tissue just beneath the bark) are aligned. Secure the graft with grafting tape or rubber bands, and apply a grafting seal to protect the cut surfaces. Keep the grafted tree in a sheltered location until the graft union has healed and new growth begins to emerge.

Successful propagation requires not only attention to the technical aspects of the process but also patience and care. Providing the right environment, including proper light, temperature, and moisture levels, is key to encouraging growth and ensuring that the new plants develop into healthy trees.

Troubleshooting Propagation Issues

Even with careful planning and execution, propagation doesn't always go as smoothly as expected. Understanding common propagation issues and how to address them can help you overcome challenges and improve your success rate.

One common issue with seed propagation is poor germination. This can result from using seeds that are not viable, planting them too deeply, or allowing the soil to dry out. Ensuring that the seeds are properly cleaned and planted at the right depth, as well as maintaining consistent moisture levels, can help improve germination rates. If germination is still poor, try using a seed-starting heat mat to provide additional warmth, which can encourage faster and more reliable sprouting.

For cuttings, the most common issue is failure to root. This can occur if the cutting is taken from a weak or unhealthy part of the tree, if the rooting medium is too wet or too dry, or if the cutting is not kept in the proper environment. Using a rooting hormone can help stimulate root development, and placing the cutting in a warm, humid location can create the ideal conditions for rooting. If the cutting is not rooting after several weeks, consider trying a different part of the tree or adjusting the moisture levels in the soil.

Grafting can present challenges, particularly if the graft union does not take. This can happen if the scion and rootstock are not properly aligned, if the graft is not securely fastened, or if the graft is exposed to harsh conditions before it has a chance to heal. Ensuring that the cambium layers are well-aligned and using grafting tape or rubber bands to hold the graft in place can improve the chances of success. Protecting the graft from extreme temperatures and keeping it in a sheltered location can also help the graft heal properly.

Addressing these common issues requires a combination of careful observation and timely intervention. By troubleshooting problems as they arise, you can increase your chances of successful propagation and grow healthy, vigorous pomegranate trees.

Best Practices for Young Plant Care

Once your pomegranate trees have been successfully propagated, providing the right care during their early stages of growth is crucial for ensuring their long-term health and productivity. Young pomegranate plants require attention to their watering, light, and nutrient needs, as well as protection from pests and environmental stressors.

Watering is particularly important for young plants, as their root systems are still developing. Keep the soil consistently moist but not waterlogged, and avoid letting the soil dry out completely. Overwatering can lead to root rot, so be mindful of the drainage in your pots or planting area. As the plants grow and their root systems become more established, you can gradually reduce the frequency of watering.

Providing adequate light is essential for young pomegranate trees. Place the plants in a location where they will receive plenty of sunlight, ideally six to eight hours per day. If growing indoors or in a greenhouse, supplemental lighting may be necessary to ensure the plants receive enough light. Insufficient light can lead to weak, leggy growth, so make sure your plants are getting the light they need to thrive.

Feeding young plants with a balanced fertilizer can help support their growth during this critical period. A slow-release fertilizer or a diluted liquid fertilizer applied every few weeks provides the necessary nutrients without overwhelming the young plants. Be careful not to over-fertilize, as this can lead to excessive vegetative growth at the expense of root development.

Pests can be a problem for young pomegranate plants, especially aphids, mealybugs, and spider mites. Regularly inspect your plants for signs of pest activity, such as discolored leaves, sticky residue, or visible insects. If pests are detected, treat them promptly with insecticidal soap, neem oil, or other organic pest control methods. Keeping the plants healthy and stress-free helps reduce their susceptibility to pests.

Protecting young plants from environmental stressors, such as extreme temperatures or strong winds, is also important. If growing outdoors, consider using a shade cloth or windbreak to protect the plants from harsh conditions. If growing indoors, ensure that the temperature remains stable and avoid placing the plants near drafts or heat sources.

By following these best practices for young plant care, you can help your pomegranate trees establish strong root systems and healthy growth, setting them up for a productive and fruitful future. Proper attention during this early stage ensures that your plants have the foundation they need to thrive for years to come.

Chapter 12

Growing Pomegranates in Containers

Growing pomegranates in containers is an excellent option for gardeners with limited space or those who live in climates where pomegranates cannot be grown outdoors year-round. Container gardening allows for greater control over soil conditions, watering, and exposure to sunlight, making it possible to cultivate healthy and productive pomegranate trees even on patios, balconies, or small gardens.

Selecting the Right Container

Choosing the right container is the first crucial step in successfully growing pomegranates in a confined space. Pomegranates have a robust root system that requires ample space to grow, so the container must be large enough to accommodate this growth. A container with a capacity of at least 15 to 20 gallons is recommended for a mature pomegranate tree. This size ensures that the roots have sufficient room to spread, which is essential for the overall health and stability of the tree.

Material is another important consideration when selecting a container. Containers made of clay, ceramic, or wood are popular choices because they provide good insulation and allow the roots to breathe. However, these materials can be heavy, especially when filled with soil, making them difficult to move. Plastic containers are lighter and easier to maneuver, but they may not provide as much insulation, which can lead to fluctuating soil temperatures. If opting for plastic, choose a thick, UV-resistant option to ensure durability and protect the roots from temperature extremes.

Growing Pomegranate in Containers

Drainage is a key factor in container selection. Pomegranates are highly susceptible to root rot, so the container must have adequate drainage holes to prevent water from accumulating at the bottom. Containers with multiple drainage holes are ideal, as they allow excess water to escape easily, reducing the risk of waterlogged soil. If the container you choose has limited drainage, consider drilling additional holes to improve water flow.

For gardeners who plan to move their pomegranate trees indoors during the winter, consider using containers with built-in casters or placing the container on a wheeled plant stand. This makes it easier to move the tree as needed, reducing the risk of injury to the plant or gardener. Additionally, using a container that is slightly smaller than the recommended size during the first few years can make the tree more manageable while it is still young.

Selecting the right container is essential for the successful growth of pomegranate trees in a limited space. The container should provide ample room for the roots, offer good drainage, and be easy to move if necessary.

Soil Mix and Fertilization for Container Growth

The soil mix used in containers plays a significant role in the success of growing pomegranates in confined spaces. Unlike garden soil, which may be too heavy and prone to compaction, container-grown pomegranates require a well-draining, nutrient-rich potting mix that promotes healthy root development and allows for adequate aeration.

A high-quality potting mix formulated for fruit trees or container plants is an excellent starting point. These mixes typically contain a blend of peat moss, perlite, and compost, providing the ideal balance of moisture retention and drainage. To improve the structure and fertility of the soil, consider adding additional organic matter, such as compost or aged manure. This not only enriches the soil with essential nutrients but also enhances its ability to retain moisture without becoming waterlogged.

Fertilization is crucial for container-grown pomegranates, as the nutrients in the potting mix can become depleted over time. A balanced, slow-release fertilizer with an NPK ratio of 10-10-10 or 12-12-12 is ideal for promoting healthy growth throughout the growing season. Apply the fertilizer according to the manufacturer's instructions, typically once in early spring and again in mid-summer. For an organic option, consider using compost tea or a well-balanced organic fertilizer that provides a steady supply of nutrients over time.

In addition to the regular fertilization schedule, container-grown pomegranates may benefit from supplemental feedings with a liquid fertilizer, especially during the fruiting period. Liquid fertilizers can be applied every two to four weeks, depending on the tree's needs, to provide an extra boost of nutrients that support fruit development. Be sure to follow the dilution instructions on the fertilizer label to avoid over-fertilizing, which can lead to nutrient imbalances or root burn.

Monitoring the pH level of the soil is also important for container-grown pomegranates. These trees prefer slightly acidic to neutral soil with a pH range of 5.5 to 7.0. If the pH level is too high or too low, the tree may struggle to absorb essential nutrients, leading to poor growth and reduced fruit production. Regularly test the soil pH using a home testing kit, and adjust as needed by adding lime to raise the pH or sulfur to lower it.

Watering and Drainage Considerations

Proper watering is one of the most critical aspects of growing pomegranates in containers. Container-grown plants are more vulnerable to fluctuations in moisture levels compared to those planted in the ground, so maintaining consistent soil moisture is key to their health and productivity.

Understanding the specific watering needs of pomegranates and ensuring adequate drainage are essential for preventing common issues like root rot and water stress.

Pomegranates prefer soil that is consistently moist but not waterlogged. Water the tree thoroughly, ensuring that water reaches the entire root system. The best practice is to water until water begins to drain out of the bottom of the container, indicating that the soil is fully saturated. However, it's important to allow the soil to dry out slightly between waterings to prevent waterlogging, which can lead to root rot. A good rule of thumb is to water when the top inch of soil feels dry to the touch.

The frequency of watering will vary depending on factors such as the size of the container, the type of soil mix used, the local climate, and the season. During the warmer months, pomegranate trees in containers may need to be watered more frequently, as the soil tends to dry out faster due to higher temperatures and increased evaporation. In contrast, during cooler months or periods of dormancy, the tree's water needs will decrease, and watering should be adjusted accordingly.

Ensuring proper drainage is vital for preventing water-related issues. As mentioned earlier, the container must have sufficient drainage holes to allow excess water to escape. If you notice that water is not draining properly, consider elevating the container slightly off the ground using pot feet or a plant stand to improve airflow and drainage. Additionally, avoid placing a saucer directly under the container, as this can trap water and lead to root rot.

Using mulch on the surface of the soil can help retain moisture, reduce evaporation, and regulate soil temperature. Organic mulches, such as shredded bark, straw, or compost, are excellent choices for container-grown pomegranates. Mulching also helps reduce weed growth and adds organic matter to the soil as it decomposes. However, be careful not to pile the mulch too high around the base of the tree, as this can create a breeding ground for pests and diseases.

Monitoring the moisture levels in the soil is crucial for container-grown pomegranates. Investing in a moisture meter can help you accurately gauge when to water, reducing the risk of over- or under-watering.

Tips for Overwintering Container-Grown Pomegranates

Overwintering pomegranate trees grown in containers is essential for protecting them from cold weather and ensuring they remain healthy during the dormant season. While pomegranates are generally hardy in USDA zones 7-10, container-grown trees are more susceptible to temperature fluctuations and may require additional protection in cooler climates. Properly preparing your pomegranate tree for winter can help it survive and thrive in the coming growing season.

One of the first steps in overwintering is determining whether your pomegranate tree needs to be moved indoors. If you live in a region where winter temperatures regularly drop below 20°F (-6°C), it's advisable to bring the container indoors or into a greenhouse for the winter months. Pomegranates are deciduous, meaning they will lose their leaves and enter dormancy during the winter, so they do not require as much light during this time. A cool, dark, and frost-free location, such as a garage, basement, or unheated greenhouse, is ideal for overwintering.

Before moving the tree indoors, inspect it for pests and diseases. Treat any issues before bringing the tree inside to prevent infestations from spreading to other plants. Prune away any dead or damaged branches, and remove any remaining fruit to reduce the risk of attracting pests. This also helps the tree conserve energy during dormancy.

Once indoors, water the tree sparingly. During dormancy, pomegranate trees require much less water, and overwatering can lead to root rot. Allow the soil to dry out slightly between waterings, but do not let it become completely dry. Check the soil moisture regularly and adjust your watering schedule as needed. If the tree is overwintering in a very dry environment, consider placing a tray of water near the tree to increase humidity, but avoid placing the container directly in the water.

If moving the tree indoors is not an option, or if you live in a milder climate, you can protect the tree by insulating the container and covering the tree with frost cloth. Wrapping the container with insulating materials, such as burlap, bubble wrap, or straw, helps protect the roots from freezing temperatures. Applying a thick layer of mulch around the base of the tree also provides additional insulation. Covering the tree with frost cloth or a similar material on particularly cold nights can help protect the branches and buds from frost damage.

With the right preparation and care, container-grown pomegranate trees can successfully overwinter and be ready to produce a healthy crop in the following season. Providing adequate protection from the cold and monitoring the tree's water needs during dormancy ensures that your pomegranate tree remains healthy and resilient through the winter months.

Chapter 13

Sustainable and Organic Pomegranate Farming

Sustainable and organic farming practices are becoming increasingly important as more gardeners and farmers seek to grow their crops in ways that protect the environment and promote long-term soil health. Organic pomegranate farming focuses on avoiding synthetic chemicals, using natural methods to manage pests and diseases, and adopting sustainable practices that ensure a healthy ecosystem.

Principles of Organic Farming

Organic farming is based on a holistic approach to agriculture that prioritizes the health of the soil, plants, animals, and the environment. At its core, organic farming seeks to work in harmony with nature rather than relying on synthetic chemicals and artificial inputs. For pomegranate growers, this means adopting practices that build soil fertility, enhance biodiversity, and promote a balanced ecosystem that supports healthy plant growth.

One of the fundamental principles of organic farming is soil health. Healthy soil is the foundation of a productive farm, and organic farmers prioritize practices that enhance soil fertility and structure. This includes using compost, cover crops, and crop rotations to add organic matter to the soil and improve its ability to retain moisture and nutrients. In organic pomegranate farming, maintaining healthy soil ensures that the trees have access to the nutrients they need to produce high-quality fruit.

Biodiversity is another key principle of organic farming. By encouraging a diverse range of plants, animals, and insects, organic farmers create a more resilient ecosystem that can naturally manage pests and diseases. In pomegranate farming, this can be achieved by planting a variety of cover crops, creating habitat for beneficial insects, and avoiding monoculture practices that can deplete soil nutrients and increase the risk of pest infestations.

Organic farming also emphasizes the importance of reducing waste and conserving resources. This includes practices such as composting organic waste, minimizing water use through efficient irrigation systems, and using renewable energy sources when possible. In pomegranate farming, reducing water waste is particularly important, as pomegranates are grown in many arid and semi-arid regions where water is a precious resource.

Pest Control Without Chemicals

Pest control is a significant challenge for organic pomegranate farmers, as the use of synthetic pesticides is prohibited. However, organic farmers can rely on a variety of natural methods to manage pests effectively while protecting the environment and promoting a healthy ecosystem. Integrated pest management (IPM) is a key strategy used in organic farming to control pests without relying on chemical interventions.

IPM begins with prevention, which is the most effective way to manage pests. Preventive measures include choosing pest-resistant pomegranate varieties, maintaining healthy soil, and practicing good sanitation in the orchard. Keeping the orchard clean by removing fallen fruit, pruning dead or diseased branches, and managing weeds helps reduce the habitat for pests and prevents infestations from becoming established.

Beneficial insects play a vital role in organic pest control. Ladybugs, lacewings, and parasitic wasps are natural predators of common pomegranate pests such as aphids, scale, and mealybugs. By creating a habitat that supports these beneficial insects, such as planting nectar-rich flowers and providing shelter, organic farmers can encourage natural pest control. In some cases, beneficial insects can be introduced into the orchard as part of a biological control program.

Organic farmers can also use physical barriers and traps to manage pests. Row covers, insect netting, and sticky traps can be effective at preventing pests from reaching the pomegranate trees. For example, using sticky bands around the trunks of the trees can prevent ants from climbing up and protecting aphids from their natural predators. These non-chemical methods help reduce pest populations without harming the environment or beneficial organisms.

Botanical pesticides, such as neem oil and insecticidal soaps, are permitted in organic farming and can be used as a last resort when pest populations become unmanageable. These products are derived from natural sources and have a lower environmental impact than synthetic pesticides. However, organic farmers use these treatments sparingly and only as part of an overall IPM strategy that prioritizes prevention and biological control.

Implementing pest control without chemicals requires a proactive and integrated approach that focuses on prevention, biological control, and the use of natural products. By adopting these methods, organic pomegranate farmers can protect their crops while maintaining the integrity of their farming system and the health of the surrounding environment.

Using Organic Fertilizers and Soil Amendments

Compost is a highly beneficial organic fertilizer in pomegranate cultivation.

Fertilization is a critical component of organic pomegranate farming, but instead of relying on synthetic fertilizers, organic farmers use natural sources of nutrients to promote healthy growth and fruit production. Organic fertilizers and soil amendments not only provide essential nutrients to the pomegranate trees but also improve soil health and contribute to long-term fertility.

Compost is one of the most valuable organic fertilizers in pomegranate farming. Rich in organic matter, compost improves soil structure, enhances water retention, and provides a steady supply of nutrients as it breaks down. Applying compost to the base of pomegranate trees helps build healthy soil and provides the tree with essential nutrients like nitrogen, phosphorus, and potassium. Regular applications of compost can also increase the microbial activity in the soil, promoting a more balanced and resilient ecosystem.

Other organic fertilizers, such as animal manure, fish emulsion, and seaweed extracts, are also commonly used in organic pomegranate farming. These fertilizers provide a rich source of nutrients and are often used as part of a comprehensive fertilization program that includes compost, cover crops, and natural soil amendments. Manure from animals such as chickens, cows, and horses is particularly high in nitrogen, which is essential for healthy foliage growth. However, it's important to compost manure before applying it to the trees to avoid introducing pathogens and to ensure that the nutrients are more readily available to the plants.

Cover crops are another valuable tool in organic pomegranate farming. Planting cover crops such as legumes, clover, or vetch between rows of pomegranate trees helps fix nitrogen in the soil, reduces erosion, and adds organic matter when the cover crops are turned into the soil. These "green manures" contribute to soil fertility and help suppress weeds, reducing the need for additional inputs.

In some cases, organic farmers may also use specific soil amendments, such as rock phosphate or green sand, to address nutrient deficiencies in the soil. These amendments provide a slow-release source of essential minerals like phosphorus and potassium, which are important for flowering and fruit development. By using a combination of organic fertilizers and soil amendments, pomegranate farmers can create a nutrient-rich environment that supports healthy tree growth and high-quality fruit production.

The use of organic fertilizers and soil amendments is central to maintaining soil health and promoting sustainable pomegranate farming. These natural inputs provide essential nutrients while also contributing to the long-term fertility of the soil, ensuring that pomegranate orchards remain productive for years to come.

Sustainable Practices for Long-Term Yield

Sustainable pomegranate farming is about more than just avoiding synthetic chemicals—it's about adopting practices that ensure the long-term health and productivity of the orchard. This includes strategies for conserving resources, protecting the environment, and maintaining the health of the trees over time. By focusing on sustainability, organic pomegranate farmers can produce high-quality fruit while preserving the land for future generations.

Water conservation is a top priority in sustainable pomegranate farming, especially in regions where water resources are limited. Efficient irrigation systems, such as drip irrigation, deliver water directly to the roots of the trees, minimizing waste and reducing evaporation. Mulching around the base of the trees helps retain soil moisture and reduces the need for frequent watering. In addition to conserving water, sustainable farmers also focus on improving soil health, as healthy soil retains water more effectively and reduces the need for irrigation.

Maintaining biodiversity in the orchard is another key aspect of sustainability. Planting cover crops, creating habitat for pollinators, and encouraging the presence of beneficial insects all contribute to a more resilient ecosystem. By fostering biodiversity, organic pomegranate farmers can reduce their reliance on external inputs and create a self-sustaining system that naturally manages pests and diseases.

Pruning and tree management are also important for maintaining long-term yield. Regular pruning helps improve air circulation, reduce disease pressure, and encourage the growth of new fruiting wood. Sustainable farmers prioritize gentle pruning techniques that promote the health of the tree while also maximizing fruit production. In addition, proper spacing of trees ensures that each tree has enough room to grow and access sunlight, which is essential for high yields.

Soil health is the foundation of sustainable farming, and organic farmers take a long-term approach to building and maintaining fertile soil. Practices such as composting, crop rotation, and the use of organic fertilizers help build soil structure, improve nutrient availability, and support the growth of beneficial soil organisms.

By adopting sustainable practices, organic pomegranate farmers can achieve long-term yield and productivity while also protecting the environment and conserving natural resources. These practices not only benefit the farm but also contribute to the overall health and sustainability of the surrounding ecosystem, ensuring that pomegranate farming can continue for generations to come.

Chapter 14

Maximizing Pomegranate Yield

Achieving a high yield of quality pomegranates requires more than just basic care. For those seeking to maximize their harvest, advanced techniques can make a significant difference. These methods, including strategic thinning, effective grafting, optimizing pollination, and precise pruning, can help enhance both the quantity and quality of your pomegranate crop.

Thinning Your Fruit: Why It Matters and How to Do It

Thinning is a crucial practice for pomegranate growers who aim to achieve the best possible fruit quality. The process involves selectively removing some of the developing fruits from the tree, which might seem counterintuitive at first. However, thinning allows the remaining fruits to grow larger, with better flavor and fewer blemishes, because the tree can focus its resources on a smaller number of fruits.

When a pomegranate tree sets too much fruit, the energy and nutrients that the tree can provide to each fruit are diluted, leading to smaller, less flavorful pomegranates. Additionally, an overcrowded tree is more susceptible to disease, fruit cracking, and other issues. By thinning the fruit, the tree can direct its resources more efficiently, resulting in fewer, but larger and higher-quality, fruits.

The timing of thinning is important for the process to be effective. The best time to thin pomegranates is in late spring, after the natural fruit drop has occurred but before the fruits have grown too large. At this stage, the tree has already shed some fruits on its own, and the grower can assess which remaining fruits should be kept. Ideally, fruits should be spaced about 6 to 8 inches apart on each branch, allowing sufficient room for each one to develop fully.

To thin the fruits, start by removing any that are deformed, undersized, or growing in clusters. Clusters of fruits can lead to competition for resources and increase the risk of damage from pests or diseases. Use pruning shears or scissors to carefully cut the fruit stems close to the base, avoiding damage to the remaining fruits or branches. Be mindful not to over-thin, as removing too many fruits can reduce the overall yield more than necessary.

Thinning is particularly important for young trees, which may not have the energy reserves to support a large crop. Overloading a young tree with too much fruit can lead to stress and potentially damage the tree's overall health. For older, established trees, thinning helps maintain consistent fruit quality year after year.

Thinning your pomegranate crop effectively enhances the size, flavor, and overall quality of the fruits. This simple yet impactful practice helps the tree allocate its resources more efficiently, resulting in a healthier, more abundant harvest.

Grafting Techniques to Improve Yield and Fruit Quality

Grafting is a horticultural technique that allows growers to combine the desirable traits of different pomegranate varieties on a single tree. This method not only improves fruit quality and yield but also allows for the cultivation of multiple varieties on the same tree, providing a diverse harvest. Grafting can also rejuvenate older trees, extend the lifespan of a productive tree, and introduce disease resistance.

The most common type of grafting used in pomegranates is the cleft graft, which is performed during the tree's dormant season. To begin, a scion—a young shoot or branch from a desired variety—is selected. The scion should be healthy, disease-free, and about the same diameter as the branch it will be grafted onto. The rootstock, or the part of the tree that provides the root system, should be compatible with the scion and have a healthy, vigorous growth pattern.

To perform a cleft graft, start by cutting the rootstock branch horizontally, creating a clean, flat surface. Then, make a vertical cut through the center of the branch to create a "cleft" or split. The scion is then prepared by cutting the base into a wedge shape, ensuring that the cambium layer (the green, growing tissue just beneath the bark) is exposed on both sides. The scion is inserted into the cleft, aligning the cambium layers of the scion and rootstock as closely as possible.

Securing the graft is essential for its success. The grafted area is wrapped tightly with grafting tape or a similar material to hold the scion in place and prevent moisture loss. In some cases, a grafting compound may be applied to seal the cut surfaces and protect the graft from drying out or becoming infected. Over time, the scion and rootstock will grow together, and the graft will become a permanent part of the tree.

Grafting can also be used to create multi-variety pomegranate trees, where different scions are grafted onto the same rootstock. This technique allows for the production of various types of pomegranates on a single tree, extending the harvest season and providing a greater diversity of flavors and uses.

Mastering grafting techniques allows pomegranate growers to boost tree productivity, enhance fruit quality, and create a more diverse and resilient orchard. This versatile method benefits both commercial producers and hobbyists, helping them maximize the potential of their pomegranate trees.

Optimizing Pollination for Maximum Fruit Production

Pollination is a critical factor in the successful production of pomegranate fruits. Pomegranates are primarily self-pollinating, meaning they can produce fruit with their own pollen. However, cross-pollination between flowers of different pomegranate trees can significantly enhance fruit set, size, and quality. Understanding how to optimize pollination in your orchard can lead to a more abundant and consistent harvest.

One of the most effective ways to improve pollination is by ensuring that your pomegranate trees are attracting a healthy population of pollinators, such as bees. Bees are the primary pollinators of pomegranates, and their activity can greatly increase the number of fruits a tree produces. To attract more bees, consider planting a variety of flowering plants around your pomegranate trees. Flowers that bloom throughout the growing season provide a continuous food source for bees, encouraging them to stay in the area and visit your pomegranate flowers more frequently.

In some cases, especially in areas with low bee populations, hand pollination may be necessary to maximize fruit set. Hand pollination involves manually transferring pollen from one flower to another using a small brush or cotton swab. This technique is particularly useful in small orchards or for rare pomegranate varieties where every fruit counts. Hand pollination should be done in the morning when the flowers are most receptive to pollen.

Wind can also play a role in pomegranate pollination, although to a lesser extent than insects. Ensuring that your trees are planted in a location with good air circulation can help the pollen move between flowers. However, too much wind can be detrimental, as it can cause flowers to drop prematurely or damage the delicate petals, reducing the chances of successful pollination.

The health and vigor of the pomegranate tree also influence its ability to produce and set fruit. Trees that are stressed due to poor soil conditions, inadequate water, or nutrient deficiencies may produce fewer flowers, and the flowers that do form may not develop properly. Ensuring that your trees are well-cared for with proper irrigation, fertilization, and pest management is essential for promoting healthy flower and fruit development.

Monitoring the fruit set after pollination can give you insights into the effectiveness of your pollination strategy. If you notice that many flowers are not setting fruit, it may be worth adjusting your approach, such as increasing the number of pollinator-attracting plants or trying hand pollination.

Advanced Pruning Methods to Increase Productivity

Pruning Pomegranate tree to Increase the health and productivity

Pruning is an essential practice for maintaining the health and productivity of pomegranate trees. While basic pruning techniques help shape the tree and remove dead or diseased wood, advanced pruning methods can further enhance fruit production and improve the overall structure of the tree.

Understanding the nuances of pomegranate pruning allows growers to increase yields and ensure a more consistent harvest year after year.

One advanced pruning method is known as renewal pruning, which involves regularly removing older, less productive branches to encourage the growth of new shoots. Pomegranates produce fruit on new growth, so by removing older wood, you stimulate the tree to produce fresh, vigorous shoots that will bear fruit in the following season. Renewal pruning is typically done during the tree's dormant season, late winter to early spring, before new growth begins. Focus on removing branches that are more than three years old, as these are likely to be less productive.

Another technique is selective thinning, which involves removing some of the interior branches to open up the canopy and allow more sunlight and air to penetrate the tree. Pomegranates can develop a dense canopy, which can reduce air circulation and increase the risk of fungal diseases. Thinning the interior branches helps prevent this issue while also ensuring that the remaining branches receive sufficient light to produce high-quality fruit. When thinning, focus on removing crossing or rubbing branches, as well as any that are growing inward toward the center of the tree.

Summer pruning is another advanced method that can help control the size of the tree and improve fruit quality. While most pruning is done during the dormant season, light pruning during the summer can be beneficial for managing vigorous growth. Summer pruning involves removing suckers, water sprouts, and any overly vigorous shoots that are drawing energy away from fruit production. This practice helps redirect the tree's resources toward developing the remaining fruits and can improve their size and flavor.

Training the tree to a specific shape, such as a vase or an open center, is also an important aspect of advanced pruning. These shapes allow for better light penetration and air circulation, which are critical for fruit production and disease prevention. Training the tree when it is young sets the foundation for a well-structured, productive tree as it matures. The vase shape, in particular, is popular for pomegranates, as it creates an open canopy that allows sunlight to reach all parts of the tree.

Regularly assessing the tree's growth and adjusting your pruning techniques accordingly is important to maximizing yield. Advanced pruning methods, such as renewal pruning, selective thinning, and summer pruning, allow growers to optimize their trees' productivity and ensure a healthy, bountiful harvest year after year.

Chapter 15

Problems and Solutions in Pomegranate Cultivation

While pomegranate trees are generally hardy and resilient, they can still face a variety of challenges that affect their growth, fruit quality, and overall health. From fruit cracking to fungal infections, understanding the common problems that pomegranate growers encounter and knowing how to address them is crucial for maintaining a successful orchard.

Dealing with Fruit Cracking

Fruit cracking is one of the most common issues in pomegranate cultivation, and it can be particularly frustrating for growers because it often occurs just as the fruit is nearing maturity. Cracking typically happens when the tree experiences fluctuations in water availability, causing the fruit to swell rapidly and split open. Once the fruit cracks, it becomes vulnerable to pests and fungal infections, reducing its marketability and shelf life.

Preventing fruit cracking starts with consistent watering practices. Pomegranates require regular, deep watering throughout the growing season, but sudden changes in water availability, such as heavy rainfall following a dry period, can cause the fruit to crack. Using drip irrigation systems helps maintain consistent moisture levels in the soil, reducing the risk of cracking. Mulching around the base of the tree can also help retain soil moisture and prevent sudden fluctuations.

In addition to managing water, thinning the fruit can help reduce the risk of cracking. When the tree is overloaded with fruit, the competition for resources can lead to uneven growth and increase the likelihood of cracking. Thinning the fruit early in the season allows the tree to focus its energy on fewer fruits, resulting in more uniform growth and reducing the strain on the fruit's skin.

Another factor that can contribute to fruit cracking is nutrient imbalances. Ensuring that the tree receives adequate potassium is important for maintaining the strength and elasticity of the fruit's skin. Applying a balanced fertilizer that includes potassium, as well as other essential nutrients, can help prevent cracking.

Managing Fungal Infections

Fungal infections are a common problem in pomegranate orchards, particularly in regions with high humidity or frequent rainfall. Fungal diseases, such as leaf spot, fruit rot, and powdery mildew, can affect both the foliage and the fruit, leading to reduced yields and poor fruit quality. Effective management of fungal infections requires a combination of cultural practices, environmental management, and, in some cases, the use of organic fungicides.

One of the most important practices for preventing fungal infections is proper pruning and thinning of the tree to improve air circulation. Fungal spores thrive in moist, stagnant environments, so ensuring that the tree's canopy is open and well-ventilated can help reduce the risk of infection.

Pruning away any dead or diseased branches and removing fallen leaves and fruit from the orchard floor helps eliminate potential sources of fungal spores.

Regular monitoring of the tree for signs of fungal infection is also essential for early intervention. Symptoms of fungal infections can include discolored or spotted leaves, fruit with soft, mushy spots, and a powdery white coating on the leaves or fruit. If a fungal infection is detected, removing the affected plant material and disposing of it away from the orchard can help prevent the spread of the disease.

In cases where cultural practices are not enough to control fungal infections, organic fungicides can be used as part of an integrated disease management plan. Products containing copper or sulfur are commonly used in organic farming to control fungal diseases in pomegranates. These fungicides are most effective when applied preventively, before the disease becomes widespread. Be sure to follow the application guidelines carefully to avoid overuse, which can lead to resistance and environmental harm.

Solutions for Poor Flowering and Fruit Set

Poor flowering and fruit set are issues that can significantly impact the yield of pomegranate trees. These problems can be caused by a variety of factors, including inadequate pollination, nutrient deficiencies, and environmental stressors. Identifying the root cause of poor flowering and fruit set is the first step in finding an effective solution.

One of the most common reasons for poor fruit set is inadequate pollination. Pomegranates rely on bees and other pollinators to transfer pollen between flowers, and a lack of pollinator activity can result in a reduced number of fruits. Encouraging pollinators in the orchard by planting flowering plants and providing habitat can help improve pollination rates. In some cases, hand pollination may be necessary to ensure that enough flowers are pollinated.

Nutrient deficiencies can also contribute to poor flowering and fruit set. Pomegranates require a balanced supply of nutrients, particularly phosphorus and potassium, which are essential for flowering and fruit development. A soil test can help determine if the soil is lacking in these nutrients, and applying a balanced fertilizer that includes phosphorus and potassium can help address the deficiency.

Environmental stressors, such as drought, extreme temperatures, or strong winds, can also affect flowering and fruit set. Providing consistent water, protecting the trees from harsh weather conditions, and ensuring that the trees are not stressed by pests or diseases are important steps in supporting healthy flower and fruit development.

Addressing poor flowering and fruit set requires a combination of improving pollination, ensuring proper nutrition, and protecting the trees from environmental stress. By identifying and addressing the underlying causes, growers can improve the productivity of their pomegranate trees and achieve a more abundant harvest.

How to Handle Pomegranate Pests

Pests can pose a significant threat to pomegranate trees, affecting both the health of the tree and the quality of the fruit. Common pests include aphids, scale insects, mealybugs, and fruit flies, all of which can cause damage to the tree's leaves, stems, and fruit. Effective pest management is essential for maintaining a healthy orchard and protecting the harvest.

Aphids are small, sap-sucking insects that can weaken pomegranate trees by feeding on the new growth. They are often found in clusters on the undersides of leaves or on young shoots. To manage aphids, promoting natural predators like ladybugs and lacewings is a key strategy. Introducing these beneficial insects into the orchard can help keep aphid populations in check without the need for chemical interventions. In severe cases, spraying the affected areas with insecticidal soap or neem oil can help reduce aphid numbers.

Scale insects are another common pest that can damage pomegranate trees by feeding on the sap and excreting a sticky substance called honeydew, which can lead to the growth of sooty mold. Scale insects often attach themselves to the bark, leaves, or fruit, making them difficult to spot. Regularly inspecting the tree for signs of scale infestations and pruning away heavily infested branches can help manage the problem. Horticultural oils can also be used to suffocate scale insects during their vulnerable stages.

Mealybugs are another sap-sucking pest that can weaken pomegranate trees and lead to stunted growth. Like aphids and scale insects, mealybugs excrete honeydew, which can attract ants and encourage the growth of mold. Mealybugs can be managed through regular monitoring, pruning of infested areas, and the use of insecticidal soap or neem oil. Encouraging natural predators, such as ladybugs and parasitic wasps, can also help control mealybug populations.

Fruit flies are a significant concern for pomegranate growers, as they lay their eggs inside the fruit, causing the fruit to rot from the inside out. Monitoring for fruit fly activity using traps and removing any fallen or damaged fruit from the orchard floor are important steps in preventing fruit fly infestations. In areas with high fruit fly pressure, bagging the fruit while it is still on the tree can provide physical protection from the flies.

Managing pomegranate pests requires a proactive and integrated approach that combines cultural practices, biological controls, and targeted treatments. Regular monitoring and early intervention are key to preventing pests from causing significant damage to the orchard and ensuring a healthy and productive pomegranate harvest.

Chapter 16

Troubleshooting Pomegranate Tree Issues

Pomegranate trees, while generally hardy, can sometimes exhibit signs of stress or struggle with environmental challenges. Recognizing the symptoms of stress and understanding how to address various issues are essential for maintaining a healthy and productive tree. Whether dealing with environmental stressors like frost or drought, nutrient imbalances, or reviving a struggling tree, troubleshooting is a vital skill for any pomegranate grower.

Recognizing Stress Signs in Your Tree

Understanding the signs of stress in pomegranate trees is crucial for early intervention. Trees under stress often exhibit symptoms that can be mistaken for other issues, such as pests or diseases, making it important to correctly identify the underlying cause. Common signs of stress include wilting, yellowing leaves, leaf drop, stunted growth, and poor fruit development. Each of these symptoms can indicate different types of stress, and recognizing the specific cause is the first step in addressing the problem.

Wilting is often one of the earliest signs of stress, particularly when the tree is not receiving enough water. However, wilting can also occur if the roots are waterlogged, leading to a lack of oxygen in the soil. This dual possibility means that careful observation of soil conditions is necessary to determine whether the tree is experiencing drought stress or overwatering.

Checking the moisture level of the soil before watering can prevent further damage.

Yellowing leaves, or chlorosis, can signal several issues, including nutrient deficiencies, poor drainage, or environmental stress. If the yellowing occurs uniformly across the leaves, it may indicate a lack of nitrogen, which is crucial for leaf development. In contrast, yellowing between the veins, leaving the veins green, often points to a deficiency in micronutrients like iron or magnesium. Soil testing can help diagnose the specific nutrient deficiency, allowing for targeted treatment.

Leaf drop, especially if it occurs out of season, can be a response to sudden changes in temperature or water availability. Pomegranate trees naturally shed some leaves as they prepare for dormancy, but if leaf drop occurs during the growing season, it may indicate that the tree is under stress. This could be due to a sudden cold snap, prolonged drought, or even transplant shock in younger trees.

Stunted growth and poor fruit development are often the result of prolonged stress, whether from environmental factors, nutrient imbalances, or inadequate care. These symptoms suggest that the tree's energy is being diverted away from growth and fruit production in an attempt to survive adverse conditions. Addressing the root cause of the stress is essential to restore the tree's health and productivity.

By carefully observing your pomegranate trees and recognizing the early signs of stress, you can take proactive steps to address issues before they become more serious. Timely intervention is key to maintaining a healthy orchard and ensuring that your trees continue to produce high-quality fruit.

Solutions for Environmental Stress: Frost, Drought, and Heat

Pomegranate trees are generally resilient, but they are not immune to the effects of environmental stressors like frost, drought, and extreme heat. Each of these conditions poses unique challenges, and understanding how to protect your trees from these stressors is crucial for maintaining their health and productivity. Implementing appropriate solutions can help your trees withstand environmental extremes and reduce the risk of long-term damage.

Frost is a significant concern for pomegranate trees, particularly in regions where late spring frosts can damage new growth and flowers. To protect your trees from frost, consider using frost cloths or blankets to cover them during cold nights. These materials help retain heat and prevent frost from settling on the leaves and branches. For younger or smaller trees, creating a temporary shelter using stakes and frost cloth can provide effective protection. If frost is a recurring issue, planting your trees in a location with good air circulation, such as on a slope, can help reduce the risk of frost settling around the tree.

Drought is another common environmental stressor, especially in arid regions where pomegranates are often grown. To combat drought stress, ensure that your trees receive deep, infrequent watering that encourages the roots to grow deeper into the soil, making them more resilient to dry conditions. Mulching around the base of the tree helps retain soil moisture and reduce evaporation. If water restrictions are in place, consider installing a drip irrigation system that delivers water directly to the roots, minimizing waste.

Extreme heat can also take a toll on pomegranate trees, leading to sunburn on the leaves and fruit, as well as increased water stress. Providing shade during the hottest part of the day can help protect your trees from excessive heat. This can be achieved by using shade cloth or planting companion plants that provide natural shade. Ensuring that the trees are well-hydrated before a heatwave can also reduce the risk of heat stress. Additionally, applying a light-colored, reflective mulch can help keep the soil cooler and reduce the impact of heat on the tree's root system.

Managing environmental stressors requires a combination of preventative measures and responsive actions. By protecting your pomegranate trees from frost, drought, and extreme heat, you can help them thrive in challenging conditions and ensure a healthy and productive orchard.

Managing Nutrient Imbalances

Nutrient imbalances in pomegranate trees can lead to a variety of growth and fruiting problems, making it essential to maintain a balanced nutrient supply throughout the growing season. Understanding the specific nutrient needs of pomegranates and recognizing the signs of deficiencies or excesses allows you to adjust your fertilization practices accordingly.

Nitrogen is one of the most important nutrients for pomegranate trees, as it promotes healthy leaf growth and overall vigor. However, too much nitrogen can lead to excessive vegetative growth at the expense of fruit production. Signs of nitrogen deficiency include yellowing leaves and stunted growth, while an excess of nitrogen may result in lush, green foliage with little or no fruit. Applying a balanced fertilizer with a moderate nitrogen content during the growing season helps maintain the right balance.

Phosphorus is crucial for root development, flowering, and fruit set. A lack of phosphorus can result in poor root growth, weak flowering, and reduced fruit production. Symptoms of phosphorus deficiency include dark green or purplish leaves and delayed fruit ripening. To address this, consider using a fertilizer that includes phosphorus or applying bone meal or rock phosphate to the soil.

Potassium is essential for fruit development and overall plant health. It helps regulate water balance, improve disease resistance, and enhance fruit size and quality. Potassium deficiency can lead to small, misshapen fruit and weak, spindly branches. Yellowing leaf margins and premature leaf drop are also common signs. To correct potassium deficiency, apply potassium sulfate or use a balanced fertilizer that includes potassium.

In addition to these macronutrients, pomegranate trees also require micronutrients such as iron, magnesium, and zinc. Iron deficiency, often seen in alkaline soils, leads to chlorosis, where the leaves turn yellow but the veins remain green. Magnesium deficiency can cause yellowing between the leaf veins, especially in older leaves. Zinc deficiency may result in smaller leaves, reduced internode length, and poor fruit set. Applying micronutrient-rich fertilizers or foliar sprays can help address these deficiencies.

Regular soil testing is an effective way to monitor nutrient levels and fine-tune fertilization practices. Maintaining a balanced nutrient supply ensures your pomegranate trees have the resources necessary for healthy growth and high-quality fruit production.

How to Revive a Struggling Pomegranate Tree

Reviving a struggling pomegranate tree requires a thorough assessment of the tree's condition and a targeted approach to addressing the underlying issues. Whether the tree is suffering from poor growth, lack of fruit production, or visible signs of stress, taking the right steps can help restore its health and vitality.

The first step in reviving a struggling pomegranate tree is to diagnose the problem. Start by examining the tree's environment, including soil conditions, water availability, and exposure to sunlight. Check for signs of pests or diseases that may be affecting the tree's health. Look for any physical damage to the tree, such as broken branches or wounds that could be inhibiting its growth.

Once you've identified the potential causes of the tree's decline, take action to address them. If the tree is suffering from nutrient deficiencies, apply a balanced fertilizer that includes the necessary nutrients. For trees that are water-stressed, adjust your watering practices to ensure consistent moisture levels. If the tree is dealing with pest infestations or diseases, apply appropriate treatments to manage the problem.

Pruning is another important step in reviving a struggling tree. Removing dead, damaged, or diseased wood helps the tree focus its energy on healthy growth. Thinning the canopy can improve air circulation and light penetration, reducing the risk of further disease and encouraging new growth. Be careful not to over-prune, as this can stress the tree further.

In some cases, root pruning may be necessary to encourage new root growth. This involves carefully digging around the base of the tree and trimming the outer edges of the root ball. This process stimulates the tree to produce new roots, which can improve nutrient uptake and overall health.

Providing extra care and attention during the recovery period is crucial for the tree's revival. Ensure that the tree is protected from extreme weather conditions and that it receives adequate water and nutrients. Mulching around the base of the tree can help retain moisture and improve soil health.

Reviving a struggling pomegranate tree requires patience and persistence, but with the right care, many trees can recover and return to full productivity.

Chapter 17

Expanding Your Pomegranate Orchard

Expanding a pomegranate orchard is an exciting endeavor that offers the potential for increased production and the opportunity to explore new varieties. However, planning for expansion requires careful consideration of several factors, including site selection, variety choice, and the logistics of managing a larger operation.

Planning for Expansion: What You Need to Know

Before expanding your pomegranate orchard, it's essential to evaluate your current operation and assess the feasibility of growing additional trees. Start by reviewing your existing site to determine if there is sufficient space for new trees. Consider factors such as soil quality, water availability, and sunlight exposure. If your current site cannot accommodate the expansion, you may need to explore new land or modify your existing setup to create space for more trees.

Soil preparation is a critical aspect of planning for expansion. Conducting a soil test on the new planting area will help you determine if any amendments are needed to create optimal growing conditions for pomegranates. Adding organic matter, adjusting pH levels, and ensuring proper drainage are all important steps in preparing the soil for new trees. If the soil quality is poor or the site is prone to waterlogging, consider raised beds or mounded rows to improve conditions.

Water availability is another key consideration. Expanding your orchard will increase the demand for water, so it's important to assess whether your existing water supply can meet the needs of the additional trees. Installing an efficient irrigation system, such as drip irrigation, can help manage water use and ensure that each tree receives the appropriate amount of water. If water resources are limited, consider implementing water conservation practices, such as mulching and rainwater harvesting, to supplement your supply.

Once you've assessed the site and addressed any potential challenges, develop a timeline for planting and caring for the new trees. This includes determining the best time for planting, which is typically during the dormant season, and planning for ongoing maintenance, such as pruning, fertilization, and pest management. Having a clear plan in place helps ensure a smooth transition as you expand your orchard.

Careful planning is the foundation of a successful orchard expansion. By thoroughly evaluating your site, preparing the soil, and ensuring adequate water resources, you can set the stage for a productive and thriving pomegranate orchard.

Selecting Additional Varieties for a Diverse Orchard

Expanding your pomegranate orchard offers the opportunity to diversify the varieties you grow, which can enhance your harvest in several ways. Planting a mix of pomegranate varieties can extend your harvest season, improve cross-pollination, and cater to different market preferences.

Selecting the right varieties for your orchard requires careful consideration of factors such as climate, disease resistance, and fruit quality.

One of the main advantages of growing multiple varieties is the ability to extend the harvest season. Different pomegranate varieties ripen at different times, so by planting early, mid, and late-season varieties, you can spread out your harvest and reduce the workload during peak season. For example, early varieties like 'Early Wonderful' may ripen several weeks before mid-season varieties like 'Wonderful,' while late-season varieties like 'Parfianka' can extend the harvest into late fall.

Disease resistance is another important factor to consider when selecting additional varieties. Some pomegranate varieties are more resistant to common diseases, such as leaf spot and fruit rot, which can help reduce the need for chemical interventions and improve overall orchard health. Researching the disease resistance of different varieties and selecting those that are well-suited to your local growing conditions can help prevent future problems.

Fruit quality and market preferences are also key considerations. Different varieties of pomegranates have varying levels of sweetness, tartness, and seed hardness, which can appeal to different consumer tastes. For example, some consumers prefer the sweet, soft-seeded fruit of varieties like 'Eversweet,' while others may prefer the tart flavor and firm seeds of 'Ariana.' Understanding your target market and selecting varieties that cater to their preferences can help you maximize your sales potential.

When selecting additional varieties, it's also important to consider the potential for cross-pollination. While pomegranates are self-pollinating, cross-pollination between different varieties can enhance fruit set and improve overall yield. Planting complementary varieties that bloom at the same time can encourage cross-pollination and result in larger, more consistent fruit.

Managing a Larger Pomegranate Operation

Expanding your pomegranate orchard comes with the added responsibility of managing a larger operation, which requires careful planning and organization. As the size of your orchard grows, so do the demands on your time, resources, and labor. Implementing efficient management practices is essential for maintaining the health of your trees and maximizing your harvest.

One of the key challenges of managing a larger orchard is labor management. As your operation expands, you may need to hire additional workers to help with tasks such as planting, pruning, harvesting, and pest control. Developing a clear schedule and assigning tasks to specific workers helps ensure that everything is done in a timely and efficient manner. Providing training on best practices for pomegranate cultivation can also improve the quality of work and reduce the risk of mistakes.

Automation can play a significant role in managing a larger orchard more efficiently. For example, automated irrigation systems can help ensure that all trees receive consistent water without the need for manual watering.

Similarly, using mechanized equipment for tasks such as pruning or harvesting can reduce labor costs and increase efficiency. Investing in technology that streamlines operations allows you to focus on other aspects of orchard management, such as marketing and sales.

Keeping accurate records is another important aspect of managing a larger operation. Tracking information such as planting dates, fertilizer applications, and pest control measures helps you make informed decisions and identify patterns that can improve future yields. Using farm management software can simplify record-keeping and provide valuable insights into the performance of your orchard over time.

As your orchard grows, pest and disease management becomes more complex. Regular monitoring and early intervention are essential for preventing small issues from becoming major problems. Developing an integrated pest management (IPM) plan that includes cultural practices, biological controls, and targeted treatments helps protect your trees and reduce the need for chemical interventions.

Marketing and Selling Your Pomegranates

Building a Thriving Pomegranate Business for Success

Expanding your pomegranate orchard offers the potential for increased sales, but it also requires a solid marketing and sales strategy to ensure that your harvest finds its way to consumers. Understanding your target market, developing a strong brand, and exploring different sales channels are all essential components of a successful marketing plan for your pomegranate business.

The first step in marketing your pomegranates is identifying your target market. Are you selling directly to consumers at farmers' markets, or are you targeting wholesalers and retailers? Understanding the preferences and buying habits of your target market can help you tailor your marketing efforts to meet their needs. For example, consumers at farmers' markets may be more interested in organic or specialty varieties, while wholesalers may prioritize consistent quality and large quantities.

Developing a strong brand for your pomegranate business helps differentiate your products from competitors and build loyalty among customers. This includes creating a recognizable logo, designing attractive packaging, and telling the story of your orchard. Highlighting the unique qualities of your pomegranates, such as their flavor, health benefits, or sustainable growing practices, can help attract customers and build your brand's reputation.

Exploring different sales channels is another important aspect of selling your pomegranates. In addition to direct sales at farmers' markets or through your own farm stand, consider selling to local grocery stores, restaurants, or online. Partnering with retailers or wholesalers can help you reach a larger audience and increase your sales volume. If you're interested in selling online, setting up an e-commerce platform or working with online marketplaces can provide access to customers beyond your local area.

Marketing your pomegranates also involves building relationships with your customers and providing excellent customer service. Offering samples, sharing recipes, and educating consumers about the health benefits of pomegranates can help create a positive experience and encourage repeat business. Engaging with customers on social media and through email marketing allows you to stay connected and keep them informed about your products.

Chapter 18

The Health Benefits of Pomegranates

Pomegranates have been celebrated for their health benefits for centuries, earning them a reputation as a superfood in modern times. Packed with antioxidants, vitamins, and minerals, pomegranates offer a wide range of health benefits, from supporting heart health to reducing the risk of certain cancers.

Antioxidant Properties and Their Impact on Health

Pomegranates are rich in antioxidants, which are compounds that help protect the body from oxidative stress and free radical damage. Free radicals are unstable molecules that can damage cells and contribute to the aging process and the development of chronic diseases such as cancer and heart disease. Antioxidants neutralize these free radicals, reducing their harmful effects and promoting overall health.

One of the most potent antioxidants found in pomegranates is punicalagin, a polyphenol that is unique to this fruit. Punicalagin has been shown to have powerful anti-inflammatory and anti-cancer properties, making it one of the key contributors to the health benefits of pomegranates. In addition to punicalagin, pomegranates are also rich in other antioxidants, including vitamin C, vitamin E, and flavonoids, all of which play important roles in protecting the body from oxidative damage.

The high antioxidant content of pomegranates has been linked to several specific health benefits, including improved skin health. Antioxidants help protect the skin from damage caused by UV radiation and environmental pollutants, reducing the appearance of wrinkles, fine lines, and other signs of aging. Regular consumption of pomegranates can help promote a more youthful complexion and protect the skin from premature aging.

Antioxidants also play a crucial role in supporting the immune system. By reducing inflammation and oxidative stress, pomegranates help strengthen the body's natural defense mechanisms, making it easier to fight off infections and illnesses. Studies have shown that the antioxidants in pomegranates can boost the production of immune cells and enhance their ability to protect the body from harmful pathogens.

Incorporating antioxidant-rich foods like pomegranates into your diet can have a profound impact on your overall health and well-being. The protective effects of these compounds help reduce the risk of chronic diseases, support healthy aging, and promote a stronger immune system, making pomegranates a valuable addition to a balanced diet.

Pomegranates and Heart Health

One of the most well-documented health benefits of pomegranates is their positive impact on heart health. The antioxidants, particularly punicalagin, found in pomegranates have been shown to reduce inflammation in the blood vessels, improve cholesterol levels, and lower blood pressure, all of which contribute to a healthier cardiovascular system. Regular consumption of pomegranates can help protect against heart disease, the leading cause of death worldwide.

Pomegranates have been shown to improve cholesterol profiles by reducing LDL (bad) cholesterol levels and increasing HDL (good) cholesterol levels. LDL cholesterol is known to contribute to the buildup of plaque in the arteries, leading to a condition called atherosclerosis, which can increase the risk of heart attacks and strokes. The antioxidants in pomegranates help prevent the oxidation of LDL cholesterol, reducing its ability to form plaque and keeping the arteries clear.

In addition to improving cholesterol levels, pomegranates have been shown to lower blood pressure, another important factor in heart health. High blood pressure puts extra strain on the heart and blood vessels, increasing the risk of heart disease and stroke. The polyphenols in pomegranates help relax the blood vessels, improving blood flow and reducing blood pressure. Studies have found that drinking pomegranate juice regularly can lead to significant reductions in both systolic and diastolic blood pressure.

The anti-inflammatory properties of pomegranates also play a role in protecting heart health. Chronic inflammation is a major contributor to heart disease, as it can lead to the development of plaques in the arteries and damage to the heart muscle. The antioxidants in pomegranates help reduce inflammation throughout the body, protecting the heart and reducing the risk of cardiovascular events.

Incorporating pomegranates into your diet is a delicious and natural way to support heart health. Whether enjoyed as fresh fruit, juice, or in other forms, the cardiovascular benefits of pomegranates make them a valuable ally in the fight against heart disease.

The Role of Pomegranates in Cancer Prevention

Emerging research suggests that pomegranates may play a role in cancer prevention, thanks to their high concentration of antioxidants and anti-inflammatory compounds. Studies have shown that pomegranates can inhibit the growth of cancer cells and reduce the risk of certain types of cancer, including breast, prostate, and colon cancer. While more research is needed to fully understand the extent of these benefits, the findings so far are promising.

One of the ways pomegranates help prevent cancer is by inhibiting the proliferation of cancer cells. The polyphenols in pomegranates have been shown to interfere with the growth signals that cancer cells rely on to multiply. In breast cancer, for example, pomegranate extract has been found to block the production of estrogen, a hormone that can fuel the growth of certain types of breast cancer cells. Similarly, in prostate cancer, pomegranate juice has been shown to slow the progression of the disease and reduce the levels of prostate-specific antigen (PSA), a marker of prostate cancer.

Pomegranates also have anti-inflammatory properties that can help reduce the risk of cancer. Chronic inflammation is known to contribute to the development of cancer by creating an environment that promotes the growth and spread of cancer cells. The antioxidants in pomegranates help reduce inflammation in the body, lowering the risk of cancer and other chronic diseases.

In addition to their direct effects on cancer cells, pomegranates can also help protect against the damage caused by carcinogens, substances that can trigger the development of cancer. The antioxidants in pomegranates help neutralize free radicals, which can damage DNA and lead to the formation of cancer cells. By protecting the body from oxidative stress, pomegranates help reduce the risk of cancer and promote overall health.

While no single food can guarantee cancer prevention, incorporating pomegranates into a balanced diet is a delicious and natural way to support your body's defenses against cancer. The potent combination of antioxidants, anti-inflammatory compounds, and other nutrients found in pomegranates makes them a valuable addition to any cancer-prevention strategy.

Incorporating Pomegranates into a Healthy Diet

Incorporating pomegranates into your daily diet is a simple and delicious way to boost your intake of essential nutrients and antioxidants. Whether enjoyed fresh, juiced, or in various preserved forms, pomegranates offer a versatile and flavorful addition to a wide range of dishes, from breakfast to dinner and everything in between.

One of the easiest ways to incorporate pomegranates into your diet is by adding the arils to salads. The sweet-tart flavor of pomegranate seeds pairs beautifully with greens, nuts, and cheeses, adding a burst of flavor and texture to any salad. For a simple yet nutritious lunch, try combining pomegranate arils with mixed greens, goat cheese, walnuts, and a light vinaigrette.

Pomegranates can also be incorporated into breakfast dishes for a nutritious start to the day. Sprinkle fresh pomegranate seeds over oatmeal, yogurt, or smoothie bowls for added sweetness and a boost of antioxidants. Pomegranate juice can be used as a base for smoothies, providing a tangy, refreshing flavor that complements a wide range of fruits and vegetables.

For those who enjoy cooking, pomegranate syrup can be used to glaze meats, create marinades, or add depth to sauces. Its rich, complex flavor enhances everything from roasted vegetables to grilled meats, making it a versatile ingredient in both savory and sweet dishes. Pomegranate molasses, a thicker, more concentrated form of pomegranate syrup, is a staple in Middle Eastern cuisine and can be used to add a tangy-sweet flavor to stews, salads, and dips.

Pomegranates also make a delicious and healthy snack on their own. Enjoy fresh pomegranate seeds as a quick and easy snack, or freeze them for a cool treat on a hot day. Dried pomegranate arils can be added to trail mix, energy bars, or baked goods, providing a convenient way to enjoy the health benefits of pomegranates on the go.

Incorporating pomegranates into your diet is not only a delicious way to enjoy their unique flavor but also a powerful tool for promoting overall health and well-being. With so many ways to use pomegranates, this versatile fruit can easily become a staple in your healthy eating routine.

Chapter 19

Pomegranate Recipes for Every Occasion

Pomegranates bring vibrant color, a burst of flavor, and a wealth of nutrients to any dish, making them a versatile ingredient that can be incorporated into meals from morning to night. Whether you are preparing a refreshing breakfast, a bold main course, a sweet indulgence, or a sophisticated beverage, pomegranates offer endless possibilities for creating delicious and visually stunning dishes. Embrace the versatility of this remarkable fruit with these pomegranate-inspired recipes that are perfect for any occasion.

Breakfast Ideas: Pomegranate Smoothies and Bowls

Starting your day with pomegranates is an easy way to add a nutritious boost to your breakfast routine. Pomegranate smoothies are a vibrant and refreshing option that can be customized to suit your taste. Begin by blending fresh pomegranate juice with frozen berries, a banana for creaminess, and a spoonful of yogurt or a plant-based alternative. This combination creates a smoothie that is not only packed with antioxidants but also provides a satisfying balance of flavors. To add more texture, consider tossing in a handful of spinach or kale for an extra dose of greens, or boost the protein content with a scoop of your favorite protein powder.

Smoothie bowls are another breakfast favorite that can be easily transformed with the addition of pomegranate arils. Create a thicker smoothie base by blending frozen fruits, such as bananas or mangoes, with pomegranate juice. Pour the mixture into a bowl and top it with a variety of colorful and nutritious toppings. Fresh pomegranate seeds add a bright pop of color and a burst of juicy flavor that contrasts beautifully with ingredients like granola, coconut flakes, chia seeds, and sliced almonds. For a more indulgent twist, drizzle honey or pomegranate syrup over the top.

Pomegranate Smoothies and Bowls

Overnight oats with pomegranate seeds are a great option for busy mornings. Simply mix rolled oats with milk or a dairy-free alternative, add a spoonful of chia seeds, and let the mixture soak in the refrigerator overnight. In the morning, stir in fresh pomegranate arils and top with your favorite fruits, nuts, and a drizzle of maple syrup. The combination of creamy oats and juicy pomegranate seeds creates a satisfying and nourishing breakfast that requires minimal effort.

Pomegranates also pair well with yogurt parfaits. Layer Greek yogurt with pomegranate seeds, granola, and a touch of honey for a deliciously creamy and crunchy breakfast. The sweet-tart flavor of the pomegranate balances the richness of the yogurt, while the granola adds a satisfying crunch. This parfait is perfect for a quick and healthy breakfast or as an afternoon snack.

With so many options for incorporating pomegranates into your breakfast, it's easy to start your day on a nutritious and flavorful note. These recipes offer a variety of textures, colors, and tastes that make breakfast an enjoyable and energizing experience.

Main Courses: Salads, Sauces, and Marinades

Pomegranates bring a unique sweet-tart flavor that can elevate any main course, from light salads to hearty entrees. Pomegranate arils add a delightful crunch and burst of flavor to salads, making them an ideal topping for leafy greens, grains, and roasted vegetables. One classic combination is a salad of mixed greens, pomegranate seeds, crumbled goat cheese, and toasted walnuts, all tossed in a light vinaigrette made with pomegranate syrup, olive oil, and balsamic vinegar. The balance of flavors—sweet, tangy, creamy, and nutty—makes this salad a standout dish for lunch or as a starter at dinner parties.

For a heartier main course, consider incorporating pomegranate into sauces and marinades. Pomegranate molasses, with its rich, concentrated flavor, is the perfect base for a glaze or marinade for meats like chicken, lamb, or pork. Mix pomegranate molasses with garlic, ginger, soy sauce, and a touch of honey to create a flavorful marinade that adds depth to grilled or roasted meats. The natural sugars in the pomegranate molasses caramelize beautifully during cooking, resulting in a sweet and savory crust that enhances the overall dish.

Grain bowls are another great way to incorporate pomegranates into your main courses. Start with a base of quinoa, farro, or brown rice, and layer it with roasted vegetables, pomegranate seeds, and a protein source like grilled chicken, salmon, or tofu. A drizzle of tahini or a pomegranate vinaigrette ties everything together, adding richness and flavor. The combination of warm grains, fresh pomegranate arils, and a flavorful dressing creates a satisfying and nutritious meal that's perfect for lunch or dinner.

Pomegranate seeds can also be used as a garnish for soups, adding a pop of color and a burst of freshness. They pair particularly well with creamy soups like butternut squash or carrot ginger soup, where the bright flavor of the pomegranate contrasts with the richness of the soup. Sprinkle a handful of pomegranate arils over each bowl just before serving to elevate the presentation and flavor of the dish.

Whether used as a topping, sauce, or marinade, pomegranates bring bold flavors and vibrant color to main courses, making them a versatile ingredient that can transform a meal into something truly special. These dishes showcase the fruit's ability to enhance both simple and complex flavors in creative ways.

Desserts: Pomegranate Cheesecake, Sorbet, and More

Pomegranate cheesecake

Pomegranates are a perfect addition to desserts, where their bright flavor can add a refreshing contrast to rich and sweet treats. Pomegranate cheesecake is a show-stopping dessert that combines the creamy richness of traditional cheesecake with the tangy sweetness of pomegranate. A swirl of pomegranate syrup or fresh pomegranate arils folded into the cheesecake batter adds a burst of flavor and a beautiful visual effect. Top the finished cheesecake with a drizzle of pomegranate syrup and a scattering of fresh seeds for an elegant presentation.

For a lighter option, pomegranate sorbet offers a refreshing and palate-cleansing dessert that's perfect after a rich meal. To make pomegranate sorbet, combine fresh pomegranate juice with a simple syrup made from sugar and water, then freeze the mixture in an ice cream maker. The result is a vibrant, jewel-toned sorbet with a bright, tart flavor that's both satisfying and refreshing. Serve the sorbet on its own or pair it with a few fresh pomegranate seeds for added texture.

Another simple yet delightful dessert is pomegranate parfaits. Layer whipped cream or mascarpone cheese with pomegranate seeds and crushed graham crackers or shortbread cookies for a no-bake dessert that's both easy to make and visually stunning. The combination of creamy, crunchy, and juicy elements creates a dessert that's satisfying without being overly heavy.

Pomegranates can also be used to create beautiful and flavorful tarts. A pomegranate tart with a buttery pastry crust, a layer of silky pastry cream, and a topping of fresh pomegranate arils is both visually impressive and delicious. The tartness of the pomegranate complements the richness of the pastry cream, while the crisp crust provides a satisfying contrast in texture.

Chocolate lovers can incorporate pomegranates into truffles or brownies for a unique twist on classic desserts. Pomegranate arils can be folded into brownie batter or added to the filling of chocolate truffles, where their bright flavor adds a surprising and delightful contrast to the deep richness of the chocolate. The combination of sweet, tart, and bitter elements creates a sophisticated dessert that's perfect for special occasions.

Whether you're looking for a light and refreshing dessert or something more indulgent, pomegranates can add a unique and delicious element to a wide range of sweet treats. Their versatility makes them an excellent ingredient for creative and memorable desserts that will impress your guests.

Beverages: Pomegranate Cocktails and Mocktails

Pomegranates add vibrant color and refreshing flavor to beverages, making them a popular choice for both cocktails and mocktails. Pomegranate juice and syrup can be used as a base for a wide variety of drinks, from simple spritzers to complex cocktails, offering endless possibilities for creative and delicious beverages that are perfect for any occasion.

Pomegranate martinis are a sophisticated and festive cocktail option that combines vodka, pomegranate juice, and a splash of orange liqueur. The result is a vibrant, tangy drink with a perfect balance of sweetness and acidity. Garnish with a twist of lemon or a few fresh pomegranate seeds for an elegant presentation. This cocktail is ideal for holiday parties or any celebration where a touch of sophistication is desired.

For a refreshing non-alcoholic option, pomegranate spritzers are a great choice. Simply mix pomegranate juice with sparkling water and a squeeze of fresh lime for a light and fizzy beverage that's perfect for summer gatherings or as a refreshing accompaniment to a meal. Add a few mint leaves and a slice of lime for a touch of elegance and extra flavor. Pomegranate spritzers are easy to customize with different flavor combinations, such as adding a splash of ginger syrup or fresh berries for added complexity.

Margarita lovers can enjoy a pomegranate twist on the classic cocktail. Replace the lime juice in a traditional margarita with pomegranate juice, and mix it with tequila, triple sec, and a splash of lime. The result is a tart and tangy margarita with a vibrant color that's sure to impress. Rim the glass with salt or sugar, and garnish with a slice of lime and a few pomegranate seeds for a festive touch.

For a warm and comforting drink during the colder months, pomegranate mulled cider is a delicious option. Combine apple cider, pomegranate juice, cinnamon sticks, cloves, and a splash of orange juice in a pot and simmer until fragrant. This spiced drink is perfect for holiday gatherings or cozy evenings by the fire, offering a warm and aromatic blend of flavors that's sure to please.

Pomegranate cocktails and mocktails are not only delicious but also visually stunning, making them the perfect addition to any gathering. With their bold color and refreshing flavor, pomegranates bring a touch of elegance and sophistication to any beverage.

Chapter 20

Additional Resources

Glossary of Terms Specific to Pomegranate Terminology

Understanding the specific terminology related to pomegranate cultivation is important for effectively communicating and implementing best practices. This glossary provides clear definitions of key terms that every pomegranate grower should know:

1. **Arils**: The juicy, edible seed coverings found inside pomegranates. These arils contain the pomegranate's seeds and are the part of the fruit that is most commonly eaten.

2. **Deciduous**: Refers to trees or plants that shed their leaves annually. Pomegranate trees are deciduous, meaning they lose their leaves during the winter months.

3. **Dormancy**: The period in a pomegranate tree's life cycle when growth slows or stops, typically during the winter season. Dormancy is a time of rest and conservation of energy for the tree.

4. **Punicalagins**: A type of antioxidant found in pomegranates that contributes to their health benefits. Punicalagins are unique to pomegranates and are responsible for much of the fruit's high antioxidant content.

5. **Graft Union**: The point where a scion (a young shoot or twig) is grafted onto the rootstock of another tree. Successful grafting requires the cambium layers of the scion and rootstock to fuse together.

6. **Suckers**: Unwanted shoots that grow from the base of a pomegranate tree or from its roots. Suckers can divert nutrients from the main tree and should be removed to encourage healthy growth.

7. **Cross-Pollination**: The transfer of pollen from the flowers of one pomegranate tree to another, which can enhance fruit set and improve yield. While pomegranates are self-pollinating, cross-pollination can still offer benefits.

8. **Fruiting Wood**: The branches on a pomegranate tree that produce flowers and, subsequently, fruit. Pruning to encourage the growth of new fruiting wood is essential for maintaining a productive tree.

This glossary offers a quick reference for understanding pomegranate-specific terminology, helping you navigate the complexities of growing and caring for these unique trees.

Troubleshooting List & Quick Fixes for Common Problems

Even experienced pomegranate growers encounter challenges from time to time. This troubleshooting list provides solutions to some of the most common problems you might face, along with quick fixes to keep your trees healthy and productive.

1. **Problem**: Fruit Cracking
   Solution: Ensure consistent watering to avoid sudden changes in soil moisture. Use mulch to retain moisture and protect the roots from temperature fluctuations that can cause the fruit to swell too rapidly.

2. **Problem**: Yellowing Leaves (Chlorosis)
   Solution: Test the soil for nutrient deficiencies, particularly nitrogen, iron, or magnesium. Apply a balanced fertilizer or specific micronutrient treatments based on the results. Ensure the soil pH is suitable for pomegranates (slightly acidic to neutral).

3. **Problem**: Poor Flowering and Fruit Set
   Solution: Increase pollinator activity by planting companion flowers nearby and ensuring proper watering and fertilization. Consider hand pollination if natural pollination is insufficient.

4. **Problem**: Fungal Infections (e.g., Leaf Spot, Powdery Mildew)
   Solution: Prune the tree to improve air circulation and reduce humidity around the foliage. Apply organic fungicides like neem oil or copper-based treatments as needed. Clean up fallen leaves and fruit to prevent the spread of fungal spores.

5. **Problem**: Pests (e.g., Aphids, Scale, Fruit Flies)
   Solution: Introduce beneficial insects like ladybugs or parasitic wasps

to control pest populations naturally. Use insecticidal soap or horticultural oils for severe infestations. Monitor for early signs of pest activity and act promptly.

6. **Problem**: Root Rot

   Solution: Improve drainage by elevating the tree or planting it in a well-draining soil mix. Reduce watering frequency, especially in cooler, wetter months. Consider using raised beds or mounded rows if the soil remains consistently wet.

7. **Problem**: Sunburn on Leaves or Fruit

   Solution: Provide shade during extreme heat by using shade cloth or planting taller companion plants. Ensure the tree is well-watered before a heatwave to reduce the risk of sunburn. Reflective mulch can also help keep the soil cooler.

This troubleshooting guide offers quick solutions to common issues, ensuring that your pomegranate trees remain healthy and productive throughout the growing season.

Fun Fact About Pomegranate

Pomegranates have a rich history and are revered for their unique properties. These fun facts about pomegranate plants add an extra layer of appreciation for this remarkable fruit.

1. **Ancient Origins**: Pomegranates are one of the oldest cultivated fruits, with evidence of their cultivation dating back to 3000 BCE in ancient Persia (modern-day Iran).
2. **Symbolism**: Throughout history, pomegranates have been symbols of fertility, abundance, and immortality in various cultures, including ancient Greece, Egypt, and India.
3. **Superfruit Status**: Pomegranates are often referred to as a "superfruit" due to their high levels of antioxidants, particularly punicalagins and anthocyanins, which are believed to provide numerous health benefits.
4. **Mythological Connections**: In Greek mythology, the pomegranate is linked to the story of Persephone and Hades. Eating the seeds of the pomegranate forced Persephone to spend part of each year in the underworld, explaining the changing seasons.
5. **Variety of Uses**: Pomegranate seeds, juice, and syrup are used in a wide range of culinary applications, from salads and desserts to marinades and cocktails. The versatility of the fruit makes it a favorite ingredient around the world.
6. **Cultural Celebrations**: In Armenia, the pomegranate is celebrated as a symbol of life and fertility. It is often featured in art and used in ceremonies, especially during the New Year.

7. **A Unique Pollination Method**: Pomegranates are primarily self-pollinating, but they can also benefit from cross-pollination by bees, which can increase fruit size and yield.

These fun facts highlight the pomegranate's cultural significance, health benefits, and unique characteristics, deepening your connection to this ancient and revered fruit.

FAQ Related to Pomegranate Treatment

New and experienced growers alike often have questions about the best practices for caring for pomegranate trees. This FAQ section addresses some of the most common questions related to pomegranate treatment.

How often should I water my pomegranate tree?

Watering frequency depends on the tree's age, the season, and the climate. Newly planted trees require regular watering to establish their roots, while mature trees need deep watering every 7 to 10 days during the growing season. In cooler months, reduce watering frequency.

What is the best time to prune a pomegranate tree?

The ideal time to prune is during the tree's dormant period in late winter to early spring, before new growth begins. This helps shape the tree, remove dead or diseased wood, and encourage the growth of new fruiting wood.

How do I prevent fruit cracking?

Consistent watering is key to preventing fruit cracking. Avoid letting the soil dry out completely between waterings, and use mulch to retain moisture. Protect the tree from sudden changes in temperature, which can cause the fruit to expand too quickly.

What type of fertilizer should I use for pomegranates?

Pomegranates benefit from a balanced fertilizer with an NPK ratio of 10-10-10 or 12-12-12. Apply fertilizer in early spring and mid-summer. For organic options, compost, manure, or fish emulsion are effective choices.

How can I increase fruit production on my pomegranate tree?

To increase fruit production, ensure the tree is receiving adequate sunlight (at least 6 hours a day), water, and nutrients. Prune regularly to encourage new growth, and consider thinning the fruit to allow the remaining fruits to grow larger.

Why are my pomegranate leaves turning yellow?

Yellowing leaves can be a sign of nutrient deficiencies, particularly nitrogen, iron, or magnesium. It can also indicate overwatering or poor drainage. Test the soil and adjust your watering and fertilization practices accordingly.

Can pomegranates be grown in containers?

Yes, pomegranates can be grown in containers, but the container must be large enough to accommodate the tree's root system (at least 15 to 20 gallons). Use a well-draining soil mix and ensure the container has adequate drainage holes. Regular pruning and watering are essential for container-grown trees.

Final Care Checklist

To keep your pomegranate trees healthy and productive, it's important to follow a consistent care routine. This final care checklist outlines key tasks to perform throughout the year, ensuring that your trees receive the attention they need at every stage of growth.

- **Daily Tasks**:
    1. Check soil moisture levels and water as needed.
    2. Inspect the tree for signs of pests, disease, or stress.
    3. Monitor fruit development and remove any damaged or diseased fruits.
- **Weekly Tasks**:
    1. Prune suckers and water sprouts to maintain the tree's shape and encourage fruiting.
    2. Weed around the base of the tree to reduce competition for nutrients and water.
    3. Apply mulch if needed to retain soil moisture and suppress weeds.
- **Monthly Tasks**:
    1. Apply fertilizer or soil amendments based on soil test results.
    2. Thin the fruit to promote better fruit size and quality.
    3. Monitor for seasonal pests and take appropriate action if infestations are detected.
- **Seasonal Tasks**:

- o **Spring**: Prune the tree during the dormant period, apply fertilizer, and start regular watering as the weather warms.
- o **Summer**: Thin the fruit, protect the tree from heat stress, and maintain consistent watering.
- o **Fall**: Harvest the fruit, clean up fallen leaves and fruit, and reduce watering as the tree prepares for dormancy.
- o **Winter**: Protect the tree from frost, reduce watering, and apply mulch to insulate the roots.

This care checklist ensures that you stay on top of essential tasks throughout the year, helping your pomegranate trees thrive and produce an abundant harvest.

Daily, Weekly, Monthly, and Seasonal Care Tasks Summary

The care and maintenance of pomegranate trees require attention throughout the year. This summary provides a quick reference for daily, weekly, monthly, and seasonal tasks to help you manage your orchard efficiently.

- **Daily**: Monitor soil moisture, check for pests, inspect fruit development.
- **Weekly**: Prune suckers, weed, apply mulch as needed.
- **Monthly**: Fertilize, thin fruit, monitor for pests and diseases.
- **Seasonal**:
  - **Spring**: Prune, fertilize, resume watering.
  - **Summer**: Thin fruit, protect from heat, maintain watering.
  - **Fall**: Harvest, clean up, reduce watering.
  - **Winter**: Protect from frost, insulate roots, monitor for stress.

This summary provides an at-a-glance guide to the essential care tasks needed to ensure the long-term health and productivity of your pomegranate trees.

Final Tips for Long-Lasting Pomegranate Success

Achieving long-term success with your pomegranate trees requires a combination of careful planning, consistent care, and attention to detail. Here are some final tips to help you maximize your harvest and ensure your orchard remains productive for years to come:

1. **Stay Consistent**: Regular care and maintenance are key to preventing problems and promoting healthy growth. Develop a routine that includes daily, weekly, monthly, and seasonal tasks to keep your trees in top condition.

2. **Be Proactive**: Early intervention is crucial for addressing issues before they become serious. Monitor your trees regularly for signs of stress, pests, or disease, and take action promptly.

3. **Invest in Soil Health**: Healthy soil is the foundation of a productive orchard. Regularly test your soil and amend it as needed to maintain the right balance of nutrients and organic matter.

4. **Embrace Sustainability**: Sustainable practices, such as water conservation, organic pest control, and soil regeneration, not only benefit your trees but also contribute to the health of the environment.

5. **Experiment with Varieties**: Don't be afraid to try new pomegranate varieties to diversify your orchard and enhance your harvest. Different varieties offer unique flavors, ripening times, and disease resistance.

6. **Build a Support Network**: Connect with other pomegranate growers, join agricultural forums, and participate in local farming organizations to share knowledge and learn from others' experiences.

7. **Keep Learning**: Agriculture is an ever-evolving field, and there is always more to learn about pomegranate cultivation. Stay informed about new techniques, research, and best practices to continuously improve your orchard.

These final tips offer guidance for achieving lasting success with your pomegranate trees, helping you enjoy the rewards of your hard work for years to come.

Made in the USA
Thornton, CO
12/21/24 16:47:19

86d82c9c-20e8-4c10-9bfb-3b42a9b7ea94R01